COLOR ME
Yellow

FINDING YOUR VOICE IN
THE TENSION BETWEEN
GOD'S PROMISES AND
THEIR FULFILLMENT

SARAH RAQUEL GAUTIER

WESTBOW
PRESS®
A DIVISION OF THOMAS NELSON
& ZONDERVAN

WestBow Press books may be ordered through booksellers or by contacting:

WestBow Press
A Division of Thomas Nelson & Zondervan
1663 Liberty Drive
Bloomington, IN 47403
www.westbowpress.com
1 (866) 928-1240

Because of the dynamic nature of the Internet, any web addresses or
links contained in this book may have changed since publication and
may no longer be valid. The views expressed in this work are solely those
of the author and do not necessarily reflect the views of the publisher,
and the publisher hereby disclaims any responsibility for them.

This book is a work of non-fiction. Unless otherwise noted, the author
and the publisher make no explicit guarantees as to the accuracy of
the information contained in this book and in some cases, names of
people and places have been altered to protect their privacy.

Any people depicted in stock imagery provided by Getty Images are
models, and such images are being used for illustrative purposes only.
Certain stock imagery © Getty Images.

Scripture quotations are taken from The Holy Bible, English Standard
Version® (ESV®). Copyright © 2001 by Crossway, a publishing
ministry of Good News Publishers. All rights reserved.

ISBN: 978-1-9736-5302-8 (sc)
ISBN: 978-1-9736-5304-2 (hc)
ISBN: 978-1-9736-5303-5 (e)

Library of Congress Control Number: 2019901461

Print information available on the last page.

WestBow Press rev. date: 3/6/2019

To My Parents – My Priestly Trailblazers
You have stood firm with me in the tension,
as I became yellow,
as I am becoming yellow, and
as I will become yellow.

PROLOGUE:
THE MUSIC STOPPED.

When I was nineteen-years-old the music stopped. After taking piano lessons with my older brother for about a month, we realized I couldn't make my hands go in separate directions while being so close together. Our music teacher suggested I take up another instrument. So, I started playing the guitar when I was four. Secretly, I think my brother and I were both happy not to be playing the same instrument. The piano could be his thing, but the guitar would be mine.

We moved to Florida and after being on the waiting list for nearly two years, we finally were placed in the town's performing arts elementary school. I adamantly wanted to play the guitar, but they didn't teach guitar at the school and my mom forced me to play the violin. There I was, an eight year old aspiring guitar rock star with a newly rented violin tucked underneath my chin. Can you imagine a nerdier instrument?!

My parents graciously kept me in both guitar lessons and violin lessons, until I started high school when it became evident that I was excelling far more at the violin than the guitar. I had been accepted into the town's performing arts high school and the violin became my main focus. My childhood aspirations of rocking out on a stage with the electric guitar faded into the distance.

(Ironically, I never even played the electric guitar and was only a classically trained guitar player. I didn't even really know chords! But a kid can dream.)

Year after year, I grew in my passion for the violin. I auditioned and got accepted into the orchestra at my undergraduate university. I even received a scholarship to double major in violin performance. While I knew I wanted to go to law school, I also knew that music was a vital part of my life. Music was the language that spoke for me when words fell short. Playing the violin in orchestras, in competitions, and in church, became my voice.

Maybe you have something like this in your life. Maybe it's not an instrument, but there's something that you do that makes you feel like who you were always authentically designed to be. Perhaps it's when you put your lacrosse stick in your hand and you cradle the ball down the field to line up the perfect shot. Perhaps it's when you're behind a camera capturing the perfect lighting for the perfect image. Perhaps it's when you're pouring the milk into a cappuccino to design the perfect leaf in the foam for a customer. The pursuit of excellence you have for that thing is unmatched and undeterred and it becomes the way that you communicate your God-design to your world. That's your voice and the violin was mine.

But then in my second year of college, I began to feel pain in my left arm. Shooting pain in my left wrist revealed something was wrong. Numbness and tingling in my left shoulder caused red flags to go off in my mind. Something was not right. At this point, I was practicing two to three hours a day, going to two-hour long rehearsals, playing in ensembles, and participating in a violin masterclass. The hours spent with my instrument - this extension of my body - were taking a harsh toll on my left shoulder and wrist and then on my whole body.

I tried to avoid the pain for as long as I could. I kept it to myself for longer than I should. I knew I needed to see my doctor. Finally, after I admitted the pain, my doctor set up an appointment for me to see a hand specialist. My mom went with me and we had x-rays done. The x-rays didn't reveal that anything was broken, which was a good sign. They set me up to get an MRI done on my hand. They quickly uncovered that I had overexerted the tendons in my wrist causing severe inflammation. The tendonitis could heal with appropriate physical therapy and rest from playing the violin. While I am generally pretty stubborn when it comes to rest and taking care of myself, I listened and got straight to resting, physical therapy, and taking some pain medication to help.

When I went back to playing again after a couple of months, my wrist was fine, but the pain in my shoulder flared up again and became unbearable. During our spring concert, I remember nearly having to put my violin down halfway through our final piece because the pain was excruciating. Remember, I'm stubborn, so I pushed through the pain, but after that concert, I could barely lift my arm, because the pain was so severe.

I went back to the doctor and got an MRI of my left shoulder. The scans revealed a deformity in the bone structure of my rotator cuff. A "normal" rotator cuff has a smooth connection between the joints, but my rotator cuff looks like a hook. Every time I make the motion to pick up and hold my violin the hook presses into the tendons and the sack of fluids between shoulder and arm bones. This is a motion I have been doing since I was eight years old. After all of these years, that motion caused severe inflammation in my shoulder to the point that I could barely lift my arm. They told me I had bursitis, which is inflammation of the sack of fluid that protects the movement between the joints in my shoulder. Sitting on a cold bed in the examination room with a white and blue gown silenced by the image of my deformity, the doctor told me I needed to make a decision about playing the violin ever again.

He provided suggestions about potential solutions. Physical therapy, pain medication, cortisone shots, or even surgery. When they mentioned surgery, my mom and I asked the doctor about this process and the likelihood of truly fixing the problem. He told us that he would go inside the shoulder and try to shave down "the hook." There was a 50% chance that it would fix the problem in the long-term. I would not be able to play for at least six months while I recovered and underwent intensive physical therapy. My parents and I looked at the odds and decided at this point it wasn't really worth the risk.

I did get my first cortisone shot that day. The long, cold needle penetrating the space between my joints in my left shoulder. Honestly, it felt more painful than helpful in that moment. I sat there still and numb, except for a tear that welled up and ran quickly down my cheek. What did this all mean? What was my life going to look like if the shots, physical therapy, and pain medication didn't help?

I faithfully attended physical therapy and did the exercises they taught me at home. During the first few weeks, I went to physical therapy three times a week. I rested for three months before I picked up the violin again. Then, when I finally tried to pick it up, the pain quickly started to develop again. I knew nothing could help. My junior year of college was about to begin and the music stopped.

I was angry. I was confused. I was lost. And all of these emotions seemed trapped inside me. Music was my outlet and my voice. It was the only way that I knew how to communicate my authentic design. I never wanted to be a professional musician (I always wanted to be a lawyer - We'll talk more about that journey later), but I always thought music would be part of my life. I always imagined myself playing for my church's worship team. I always imagined myself going to rehearsals after work and playing concerts on the weekends. God had given me this talent and had used it so fully for ministering to His people and now this. I thought my hands were anointed for this purpose.

I asked so many questions during the season that followed. Why did You give it to me if You knew You were going to take it away? Why would You take it away like this? Why did You make me with this deformity in my shoulder? Why am I undergoing so much pain? Why? Why? Why? Countless "whys" that only led me further into questions and desperation. I didn't know much during this season, but I knew I had lost my voice. I knew that I felt like my calling was a grey foggy haze. I'd turned twenty-years-old and everything that I thought I knew about myself and my voice went completely silent.

My world turned upside down with a lack of clarity and lack of ability to communicate. I felt trapped inside this cave I dug inside of myself. I stopped sleeping well, I stopped eating well, and I started to question everything - even more than I already was accustomed to doing. I was an English literature major in undergrad, so I am trained to over analyze and criticize everything. I spent months wondering if my dream to go to law school was going to end up being a total flop too and nearly quit on my dream. Until one day, nearly a year later in my last year of college, a friend of mine reminded me of my authentic design.

We were sitting in her living room on the floor and there were crayons all over the grey coffee table. I was sulking and feeling depressed. I was struggling to articulate my feelings. She looked at me and said: "Sarah, I'm just going to color you yellow until you believe it." I was so confused by what she meant. The words seemed to make no sense to me. Until the light bulb went off and I realized that I am yellow. I thought my whole identity was caught up in that extension of my body underneath my neck for eleven years - my instrument, my voice. While that was part of me, it wasn't the whole of me. I was not designed to be this heavy grey cloud of doom. I was designed to be a bright beam of yellow that helps other people out of their grey clouds. This was my true voice and my true design. She knew that. She also knew that I had to go through my grey to fully appreciate my yellow. But it was time to be called out of the grey. It was time to be called out of the darkness into His marvelous light.

Color me yellow.
Yellow, the way this color mixes with other colors to create new shades, tones, and hues.
Yellow, the way a bright yellow umbrella provides shelter from the rain.
Yellow, the way bright yellow rain boots scamper through Spring's rain puddles.
Yellow, the way rays break through a cloud-filled day.
Yellow, the way light beams from a lighthouse as a beacon of hope for others to find their way.
Yellow, the way the sun breaks through every inch of darkness.
Color me a shade that lights the path for others who are searching to express their color.
Color me yellow.

PART 1

FINDING YOUR VOICE

You hold a powerful voice inside of you. A voice that adds color to God's canvas on Earth.

God is a master artisan painting a beautiful canvas filled with vibrant colors. We are those colors. We see the beauty of the canvas when we find our colors. Those colors release their fullest expression when we communicate with our God-designed voice.

Our lives can be an adventurous journey of self-discovery. God - the master artisan - has uniquely designed each of us and invites us to know our authentic design. And not simply to know it, but God desires for us to speak through our authentic design.

In a world where we constantly consume the voices of others, it can be tempting to mimic the voices we hear. We can easily dilute the unique color that God designed within us, when we allow other voices to become our voices. Our voices can become distorted when we allow ourselves to become parrots who repeat what we've heard, instead of speaking from what's deep inside us.

Finding our voice is first about uncovering what's inside. It's about uncovering those essential pigments that when, added together, reflect our God-design. We are not the echoes of other people's voices. We are not parrots who repeat others. We are not anyone else's color. We are uniquely designed colors and we can uncover that design inside of us. Together, we can begin to add our color to God's masterpiece.

In the journey ahead, I want to support you in finding your color - your God-designed voice. Think of me as a coach, mentor, cheerleader, guide, or close friend who will stand alongside you as you find your color. God wants to use your color to continue to paint a beautiful canvas in you, through you, and for others. I'm honored and excited to be on this journey with you.

Our journey is divided into three parts:
Part 1: Finding Your Voice
Part 2: In the Tension
Part 3: Between God's Promises and Their Fulfillment

Let me say at the outset, the adventure of self-discovery lasts a lifetime. One of the most exciting parts of finding our voices is that it's a journey of coming home to our most authentic selves and of becoming our most authentic selves. Each part of our journey will teach us how to find our voice and throughout our lives we'll find ourselves coming back to these parts.

In Part 1, we will learn to uncover our voice and establish a foundation.
In Part 2, we will learn to refine our voice through our challenges, obstacles, victories, and failures.
In Part 3, we will learn to strengthen our voice to impact and inspire others.

As we begin Part 1, we'll engage with three elements that form the foundation of our voices. These elements - our core values, mindset, and vision - are the essential pigments that define our colors. Our understanding of these elements provide a solid foundation for us as we go on the adventurous journey of finding our voices in the tension between God's promises and their fulfillment.

COLOR YOU _____

"At the center of God's deepest desire for you is divine longing to complete your transformation. God's dream for you is that you become whole and holy as you find your identity and fulfillment in mystical union with the Lord God." // David G. Benner, Desiring God's Will

God longs to fulfill the promises that He has made to you. But you may wonder, if God has told me "X" promise, then why doesn't my life look like "X" promise?

On our journey to find our voice in the tension between God's promises and their fulfillment, God is transforming us. Before we can begin to fully uncover our voice, we must begin to understand our identity in Christ. God creates space for us to understand ourselves, so that we can fully receive His promises.

Continuous Action in Progress

One of the core truths about your identity in Christ is:

> You have been transformed, you are being transformed, and you will be transformed.

The fulfillment of God's promises comes through the process of transformation. And transformation is a process of heavy and light. In this process, interruptions will happen that seem like barriers to finding your voice. You will feel chaotic, uncertain, or fearful that God's truths won't reach their fulfillment. You may ask yourself: "Am I really transforming at all?" These feelings can distract you. But never forget: the voice lives inside.

The Bible speaks of transformation as an "already, not yet" process. This "already, not yet" process means we have already been transformed even as we are being transformed although we have not yet been fully transformed. It's one of the great mysteries of faith and its mysteriousness makes it equally wondrous. How can we both be seated with Christ in the heavenly realms[1] even as we are presently sitting in a coffee shop reading this sentence? The answer: "Already, not yet."

"Do not be conformed to this world, but be transformed by the renewal of your mind, that by testing you may discern what is the will of God, what is good and acceptable and perfect."[2] These words, originally written in Greek, teach us that "be transformed" signifies continuous action in progress. So, we discover the instruction to "be transformed by the renewing of your mind" is an invitation to undergo a metamorphosis. As followers of Christ, the ongoing process of transformation means understanding and accepting that we are not who we were and we are not yet who we were designed to be. The process continues and unfolds. We become.

That's the beautiful part of the process of transformation. We are being transformed into our authentic design. "For we are his workmanship, created in Christ Jesus for good works, which God prepared beforehand, that we should walk in them."[3] Other versions of this verse call us His handiwork or His masterpiece.

Regardless of the translation, the truth is that you are made by God. The word used for "workmanship" is poiēma, a work of fabric. You are woven with the threads of God himself. The tag on the fabric of your life doesn't say "Made in [insert whatever country you were born in]", it says "Made in Christ Jesus". At a point in time in the past, you were created by God and created of God. You are being transformed into your authentic design - the workmanship of God. This is why your voice matters so much. This is why it's so important to find your voice. It's part of being transformed into your true design.

Accepting the process of transformation also means accepting the cost of discipleship. Transformation happens through discipline. Living out your God-designed self will cost you. Jesus tells a great crowd that was following him and searching for meaning in their lives:

> "Whoever does not bear his own cross and come after me cannot be my disciple. For which of you, desiring to build a tower, does not first sit down and count the cost, whether he has enough to complete it? Otherwise, when he has laid a foundation and is not able to finish, all who see it begin to mock him, saying, 'This man began to build and was not able to finish.'" [Luke 14:27-30]

Jesus did not sugarcoat the cost of transformation. He never told them that transformation was going to be rainbows and butterflies. In fact, He promises a cost. The disciplined work of slowing down and digging deep inside yourself comes at a cost. But this costly discipline - with its heavy and light - will result in you finding your voice and speaking your voice. Your voice - that color that God designed you to be - will be a color of His image to a world that needs to know that YOU are His workmanship.

The Pink Polka Dot Bean Bag Chair

I started to wrestle with God and my own authentic God-designed self in middle school. One the one hand, I behaved like the ultimate class clown seeking attention and doing my best to fit in with everyone. And on the other hand, I began asking all kinds of questions about God, faith, and my voice and identity in Christ. One night, I sat down on my pink polka dot bean bag chair (a gift from one of those Christmas party games that I would never buy myself purely because of the pink color!) wanting to hear from God about my identity. I did the thing that middle-schoolers and sometimes not so middle-schoolers do, I closed my eyes, opened my Bible, and looked down at the page believing that the words I opened to were directly from God for me. I definitely don't recommend this as a way to hear from God on a regular basis, but I think sometimes God honors our childish approach to His deep wonders.

My Bible stared back at me from Isaiah 11 saying:

> "There shall come forth a shoot from the stump of Jesse, and a branch from his roots shall bear fruit. And the Spirit of the Lord shall rest upon him, the Spirit of wisdom and understanding, the Spirit of counsel and might, the Spirit of knowledge and the fear of the Lord. And his delight shall be in the fear of the Lord. He shall not judge by what his eyes see, or decide disputes by what his ears hear, but with righteousness he shall judge the poor, and decide with equity for the meek of the earth; and he shall strike the earth with the rod of his mouth, and with the breath of his lips he shall kill the wicked. Righteousness shall be the

belt of his waist, and faithfulness the belt of his loins." [Isaiah 11:1-5]

I knew that the "shoot from the stump of Jesse" referred to Jesus, but if I'm created in the image of Christ, I knew these words were for me. These verses inspired me, because they felt so personal for me. That night I began to pray for wisdom and discernment. From that night on, I embraced those words as a promise for me and I've never stopped praying for the spirit of wisdom and discernment, the spirit of counsel and might, and the spirit of knowledge and the fear of the Lord. I've never stopped praying that God would help me judge and speak not by what I see or what I hear, but with righteousness. This prayer has empowered me with a unique vision to see unseen potential and build God's Kingdom in unexpected ways. This prayer has also come with the cost of putting me in challenging situations where I am often the only one who can discern what God seems up to. I have been on a lifetime journey of transforming into someone who consistently pursues God's wisdom and discernment. And as a result God has consistently placed me in the tension to be a voice for completely radical transformation. I have accepted that and God has always used the tension to strengthen my voice rather than silence it.

I wish I still had that pink polka dot bean bag chair. It stayed with me through college, but was one of the treasured things that wouldn't fit into my car when I moved to Boston. But to this day, I remember that pink polka dot bean bag chair as one of the great experiences I had with God where he began to reveal my color to me. I remind myself often that when I was in those middle school years of wrestling with my identity, God marked me with His words to color my words.

A Different Spirit

Let's rewind to a turning point in our history. This turning point will serve as the point of reference throughout our journey to teach us about finding our voice - our color. The turning point starts in the desert of Kadesh-Barnea on the southern border of Israel, the Promised Land. Moses led the Israelites from their enslavement in Egypt, through the Red Sea, and to the base of Mount Sinai where they received the law and instructions about how to live as God's holy nation and treasured possession. Now their fearless leader, Moses, chooses twelve chief leaders from the twelve tribes of Israel to go on an exploration mission into the Promised Land. Among the chosen were Joshua son of Nun from the tribe of Ephraim and Caleb son of Jephunneh from the tribe of Judah.

Moses gave them a list of questions to answer when they were exploring the land:

- Are the people in the land strong or weak?
- Are there a lot or a few people?
- Is the land good or bad?
- Are their cities big or small?
- Is the land fruitful or barren?
- Are there trees or not?

Throughout 40 days, these twelve chief leaders traveled throughout the whole Promised Land covering approximately 500 miles of land. They passed through historically and spiritually significant cities like Hebron, saw the descendants of Anak (the giants: Ahiman, Shehai, and Talmai), and found grapes, pomegranates, and figs to bring back to Kadesh-Barnea.

When they returned from the mission, they reported of a prosperous land flowing with milk and honey just as the Lord promised. However, they also reported that fortified walls surrounded the cities, giants from the descendants of Anak lived in the land, and other tribes of strong people dwelled there. As they spoke, Caleb interrupted the report, quieted the people, and spoke saying:

> "Let us go up at once and occupy it, for we are well
> able to overcome it." [Numbers 13:30]

The ten fearful leaders spoke from their fear, but Caleb spoke from his faith. Unfortunately, the fearful leaders insisted on their weaknesses and on the strength of the people in the Promised Land. They saw themselves as "mere grasshoppers"[4] compared to the people in the Promised Land.

This focus on fear, sent the Israelites into a whining frenzy. They complained they should choose a new leader and go back to Egypt! In despair, Moses and Aaron fell on their faces before the Israelites. Caleb and Joshua tore their clothes (a sign of sadness and frustration in this ancient culture). Then, Caleb and Joshua attempted to encourage the Israelites by saying:

> "The land, which we passed through to spy it out
> is an exceedingly good land. If the Lord delights
> in us he will bring us into this land and give it to
> us, a land that flows with milk and honey. Only
> do not rebel against the Lord. And do not fear the
> people of the land, for they are bread for us. Their
> protection is removed from them, and the Lord
> is with us; do not fear them." [Numbers 14:6-9]

Unfortunately, this passionate plea in favor of pursuing God's promises frustrated the people more and they shouted that Caleb and Joshua should be stoned! At this, the glory of the Lord appeared at the Tabernacle (a moveable tent where God met with the people and priests) and God spoke to Moses about the disbelief and rebellion of the Israelites. The Lord told Moses that disaster would come on them and He would disinherit them. But Moses interceded for the people and the Lord forgave them. Their sin was forgiven, but the consequences of their sin was not eliminated. The Lord declared that none of the ten fearful leaders or the unbelieving Israelites would be allowed to enter into the Promised Land. Out of everyone, only Caleb and Joshua would be allowed to enter into the Promised Land. The Lord recognized something special about Caleb saying:

> "But my servant Caleb, because he has a different spirit and has followed me fully, I will bring him into the land into which he went and his descendants shall possess it." [Numbers 14:24]

The fearfulness of the Israelites caused them to wander in the desert for 40 years - one year for every day they explored the Promised Land. The Lord sent a plague - much likes the plagues He sent in Egypt - that killed the ten fearful leaders. After the plague killed the ten fearful leaders, the Israelites took matters into their own hands - without guidance from God or Moses - and went to the Promised Land to confront the strong enemies in battle. The battle ended in total destruction for the Israelites.

Because the Israelites and the ten fearful leaders spoke with a voice that lacked a clear understanding of values, mindset, and vision, a journey from Mount Sinai to the Promised Land that should have taken them eleven days, took them 40 years. But Caleb spoke with a different voice. Caleb had a different spirit in him and he spoke with a powerful voice that clearly understood his values, mindset, and vision. He spoke with a voice that remained firm no matter what tension existed between God's promises and their fulfillment.

We Need Reminders

Caleb's story will serve as a reminder to us of the way that we can find our voice in the tension between God's promises and their fulfillment. In the tension, we need reminders. When we examine the natural rhythms of our lives we realize we use reminders. Reminders on our phones help us to remember to pay our bills on time. We need to do lists to remind us about assignments, errands, and work projects. We put quotes on our walls to remind us of inspirational truths. We put pictures on our lock screens, backgrounds, and walls to remember important people in our lives. So, if we need reminders in all of these ways to remember important things, how much more will we need reminders to move through the tension? As we walk through the tension, we need reminders of the promises God has spoken over us. We need reminders of the challenges we've been able to overcome through God's grace. We need reminders.

In fact, the Bible instructs us to remember. Long before the words of the Bible were written down in the form that we see them in today, the words of the Bible were told through the oral tradition. Stories were passed down from generation to generation, so people would remember who God was and what God had done for His people. These collections of stories told again and again held important lessons that God wanted people to remember. The Hebrew word for remember is "zakar" meaning to bring past events to mind in a way that causes them to impact present feelings, thoughts, and actions. The biblical command to remember is not a passive memory that floats through our mind and flees. The biblical command to remember is an active engagement with all that the Lord has done as the standard for all that He will do.

Caleb's story serves as one story of remembrance with important lessons for us to remember about finding our voice. In addition to Caleb's story, you will need your own reminders. You'll need reminders of how you're not who you were, but you're still not who you will be. You'll need reminders about your fundamental belief about the God who has made promises to you. You'll need to remember your values, mindset, and vision, like Caleb did, to sustain you through the tension.

What stories of remembrance reveal how you're transforming?
What stories of remembrance reveal who God is and what He's up to in your life?
What are the stories of remembrance you tell yourself?

Flow of the book

These reflective questions give us a great moment to pause and talk a bit about the flow of the book. The pages that lie in the journey ahead are designed for you not only to read, but also to respond. There's power in writing down your thoughts, feelings, reactions, and responses, because this will serve as a safe place for you to uncover the voice inside of you. It's a sacred space that you have the power to create as a platform for your voice to be released. I will be in the tension with you with my own journey to finding my voice, with Biblical stories to guide our understanding, and with practical exercises to help you find your voice.

One more quick note before we continue our journey:

As I was preparing to write this book, I started going through old Moleskines from when I first moved to Boston. This was a little over a year after my friend "colored me yellow" and I was still stumbling out of the grey to find my yellow. So much has changed since I first moved here. I've experienced so much. On the one hand, reading those Moleskines made me think how much has changed. On the other hand, I thought how much has stayed the same. How much my core self, core desires, and core voice are just as vibrant today as they were when I first began searching for my yellow. The voice has always been inside. I've realized just how in love with this city I still am now and just how eager I am to build God's Kingdom here. I had no idea how God would honor the voice of a 21-year-old budding law student. I had no idea how HUGE His promises would be for me. I had no idea how challenging the tension of this adventure of possessing those promises would be. I'm still in the tension. Still learning. Still growing. Still desiring. Still dreaming. Still unsatisfied with the ordinary.

My prayer is that this book would meet you and me in the tension. My prayer is that this would be part of me learning to speak with my God-designed voice. My prayer is that you would choose to believe in a God who is able to do exceedingly more than you could ever ask or imagine. My prayer is that in the same way I've discovered my color and stood alongside others to find their colors, that your color would be discovered. I pray that you would find your voice. It's inside of you. I pray that God would use my voice to speak His voice more clearly than my words could ever speak on their own. Speak, Lord. We are listening. Our voice is empty if it's not alive with Yours. Come alive to us and in us. Lead us with Your voice on this adventure. We are listening. Speak, Lord.

WHAT MAKES YOU TICK?
WHAT TICKS YOU OFF?

"Something inside me has always been there, but now it's awake." //
Rey, Star Wars: The Last Jedi

My mom taught middle school English for the majority of her 32 years of teaching. When you're teaching middle schoolers how to become critical thinkers that process involves teaching them to become reflective about their identities and their voices. Mama took her students outside to hug trees and lay in the grass looking up at the clouds, so that they could find inspiration for writing poetry. She played Natasha Bedingfield's song "Unwritten" at the beginning of the year to help them reflect on themselves and write letters introducing themselves to her. She showed Dead Poets Society's "Carpe Diem" scene to guide them in understanding the significance of their lives.

The first time I saw Dead Poets Society, the "Carpe Diem" scene mesmerized me (If you've never seen this movie, put the book down and go look up this scene on Youtube or better yet if it's still available on Netflix go watch it now.) Robin Williams is an unconventional English professor at an all-boys prep school. In the "Carpe Diem" scene, he invites the boys to follow him into a hallway. Here, they look at pictures of former young men who attend the school. Williams instructs them to lean in to look at the faces of these boys and tells them that these boys are just like them. Then, as they're all leaning in, he says in a raspy, haunting whisper: "Carpe…carpe diem boys…seize the day…make your lives extraordinary."

I love that scene! I love that movie - easily one of my top five favorite movies of all time. The refrain of "Carpe Diem" and living and creating an intentionally wonderful life is one of my life missions. It's a mission that makes me tick. It's a mission that gets me out of bed on the good days and on the grey days. It's a mission that strikes a chord in the strings of my core. When an experience resonates deeply within me, I know it's resonating because something about that experience strikes one of my core values.

> *Core Values: Guiding principles that direct the way you understand and approach your experiences*

These guiding principles become the non-negotiables that give you clarity about why things matter to you, why things frustrate you, why you move in certain directions, and why you prioritize some things and not others. They become "the why" undergirding your life. Clarity about your core values gives you clarity about your voice. They originate deep inside of you and invite you to explore your depths. This exploration is one where you align your core with God's core, identify what makes you tick and what ticks you off, and reflect on why you're struck.

A Spirit-Filtered Mentality

At our core, we carry the essence of God. When God created humanity, He breathed His breath into us. We carry the borrowed breath of God - the breath that gives us life at our very core. Exploring our core values begins with aligning our core selves with God's core self. This core alignment can happen in many ways, but the clearest way to discover God's core self comes from exploring His word. When we come to God's word with a humility to know our Creator and as a result know ourselves, our core and God's core become one.

Jesus tells the disciples in Matthew 24 that "Heaven and earth will pass away, but my words will not pass away.[5]" In the original language, "my words" is the phrase "the words of me." This is striking, because "the words" or "logoi" are a collection of words that have been gathered in the mind and spoken with a universal authority[6]. This means that the words of Jesus are not just any words. Jesus's words have authority and implications. The words of God will not pass away and Jesus will not pass away, because these words existed in the eternal beginning and will exist for all of eternity. The words of God reflect the guiding principles of the Kingdom of God. These principles will never pass away. If we can see what God values in His word, then we can begin to align our lives around principles that will never pass away. God graciously gives us a mechanism for seeing what He values, by giving us the mind of Christ.

I started drinking coffee soon after moving to Boston for law school, I went in search of the smoothest, most full body way to consume coffee: French press, Aeropress, pour-over, and finally the Chemex. My kitchen looks like a science project in the morning when I'm making my coffee in my Chemex. This contraption looks like a large hourglass beaker. With a filter in the top half holding the coffee grounds, you slowly pour hot water over the grounds to produce a smooth coffee output. Unlike a "normal" coffee maker, where the filter gets tucked away into the machine unseen, the Chemex exposes the filter. Each morning, making coffee in my Chemex, I am reminded of the significance of the filter. Without the filter the output would just be a muddled mess of coffee grounds and water. In the same way, the mind of Christ or what I like to call a Spirit-filtered mentality, functions as the filter that gathers and sorts our thoughts, so that our output - our voice - isn't a muddled mess. It takes time and attention to make coffee this way, just as it also takes time and attention to cultivate the characteristics of the mind of Christ.

When Paul writes in 1 Corinthians about us having the "mind of Christ," he's not writing about our ability to know that 2+2=4. He's speaking to us about the core processing center of our lives. He's speaking about a filter that helps us reason, discern, and understand our experiences. He's speaking to us about the core filter inside of us that processes the thoughts we gather and produces the words we speak.

> "Yet among the mature we do impart wisdom, although it is not a wisdom of this age or of the rulers of this age, who are doomed to pass away. But we impart a secret and hidden wisdom of God, which God decreed before the ages for our glory. None of the rulers of this age understood this, for if they had, they would not have crucified the Lord of glory. But, as it is written,
>
> "What no eye has seen, nor ear heard,
>   nor the heart of man imagined,
> what God has prepared for those who love him"—

These things God has revealed to us through the Spirit. For the Spirit searches everything, even the depths of God. For who knows a person's thoughts except the spirit of that person, which is in him? So also no one comprehends the thoughts of God except the Spirit of God. Now we have received not the spirit of the world, but the Spirit who is from God, that we might understand the things freely given us by God. And we impart this in words not taught by human wisdom but taught by the Spirit, interpreting spiritual truths to those who are spiritual.

The natural person does not accept the things of the Spirit of God, for they are folly to him, and he is not able to understand them because they are spiritually discerned. The spiritual person judges all things, but is himself to be judged by no one. "For who has understood the mind of the Lord so as to instruct him?" But we have the mind of Christ." [1 Corinthians 2:6-16]

Paul teaches us eight different characteristics of a Spirit-filtered mentality. Reflecting on these eight characteristics helps us align our core with God's core.

Characteristics of a Spirit-filtered mentality:

1. Distinguished. A Spirit-filtered mentality is distinguished, because it is a Spirit-given wisdom different from any temporal, earthly wisdom. [1 Corinthians 2:6]
2. Sustained. A Spirit-filtered mentality is sustained, because it is a Spirit-given wisdom that was pre-established before creation and has ongoing existence. [1 Corinthians 2:7]

3. Revealed. A Spirit-filtered mentality is revealed, because it comes from an authentic experience with the reality of Christ and an unveiling of His light in the midst of darkness. [1 Corinthians 2:8-10a]

4. Searched. A Spirit-filtered mentality is searched, because the Spirit has diligently examined and accurately understood the deep truths and principles of God, just as our own spirit does with us. [1 Corinthians 2:10b-11]

5. Received. A Spirit-filtered mentality is received, because the Spirit has been given to those who have accepted the reality of Christ and the Spirit serves as a bridge between what we see with our physical eyes and perceive with our spiritual understanding. [1 Corinthians 2:12]

6. Taught. A Spirit-filtered mentality is taught, because the Spirit communicates through spiritual instruction and not natural instruction. [1 Corinthians 2:13]

7. Discerned. A Spirit-filtered mentality is discerned, because it has vigorously and completely examined eternal spiritual truths. [1 Corinthians 2:14-15]

8. Intertwined. A Spirit-filtered mentality is intertwined, because when we possess the mind of Christ, we are perfectly knit together with and can identify His guiding principles. [1 Corinthians 2:16]

When you activate the characteristics of a Spirit-filtered mentality, you find yourself aligning your core with God's core more and more until His essence and your essence become fully united - a union always meant to exist. The core processing center of your life becomes transformed into a Spirit-filtered mentality that can discern the guiding principles of the eternal Kingdom of God. Core alignment gives you a clarity of mind that catalyzes a conviction of voice.

Finding our voices flows out of an intimate relationship with God through His word. When His words become our bread of life[7], our living water[8], our double-edged sword[9], and our lamp to our feet and light to our path[10], we begin to understand that the Kingdom of God - with its guiding principles - is inside of us[11]. This understanding guides us to an awareness that when we align our core with God's core we align with a truth that has always been inside of us. We speak the life and truth of the Kingdom of God not as something far off and futuristic, but as something presently inside of us.

Internal Tuning Forks

One of my favorite parts of an orchestral performance happens before the first piece. It's the moment where the concert master comes out, stands on the platform, and signals the oboe player to play an "A." This is the crucial moment of intonation - the orchestra getting in tune with itself. Without this crucial moment of intonation, the orchestra will be out of tune and the sound will be flawed. Without striking the right note and matching the resonating note, the orchestra forfeits the opportunity to play with an integrated sound.

Now, you aren't tuning your voice to a whole orchestra, but individual intonation is a crucial component in the process of identifying your core values. Individual intonation happens when you take the time to get in tune with yourself. Without these crucial moments of intonation, you like the orchestra, forfeit the opportunity to speak with a fully integrated voice.

Have you ever seen a tuning fork? (I bought one recently as an object lesson for a leadership training and the guy at Guitar Center said: "Talk about going old school!" And he was totally right about it being old school and we can learn a lot about finding our individual intonation by going old school.) Essentially, a tuning fork is a resonator of sound. But sound only resonates from the tuning fork when the tuning fork is struck and placed on a surface.

We have a tuning fork inside our core. This tuning fork resonates sound that becomes our voice, but it must be struck. So, in order for us to have those crucial moments of individual intonation, we must identify when experiences strike our internal tuning fork. The striking of those experiences either cause resonance or dissonance within us. Identifying that resonance or dissonance requires us to listen carefully. Good listeners cultivate an ear for both the internal pitch - core value - and why things resonate with that internal pitch - core value. This requires keen observation of what makes us tick and what ticks us off. If we can identify why an experience struck us, then we can identify our core values.

Marginal Pass

During my first semester of law school, I found myself struggling through Civil Procedure. Civil Procedure is THE foundational class about how to bring a civil claim to court. Not understanding this class is like saying you will fail at being a lawyer. My struggle signaled a failing coming my way. I blamed my struggle on everything: the professor spoke to fast, the professor never answered anyone's question, the cases were confusing, and on and on. Let's get real though, my lack of understanding Civil Procedure fell on me. I gave up on Civil Procedure before even trying.

In law school, you only get one opportunity to prove yourself for your grade; one cumulative test at the end of the semester determines whether or not you sufficiently understood the information. Every year, our law school gave first year students a practice exam in one of our classes to help prepare us for the rigors of law school exams. This year the practice test was in Civil Procedure. Of course the practice test was on Civil Procedure! Of course I was going to fail! I might as well quit law school now! I tanked the practice test. Predictably. This should have been a sign to me. I had the opportunity to start seizing this class with the same passion that I seized my other classes. Instead, I dug my heels in further and Civil Procedure seemed like an insurmountable giant and I was a "mere grasshopper."[12]

At the end of semester, with final exam week around the corner, I was terrified about my Civil Procedure exam. I prepared an extensive outline, I studied, and I studied some more. The day of the exam came. It was a four hour in-class exam. Right after finishing this exam, I was getting on a plane to head home to Florida for Christmas - my bags packed watching me from the side of the classroom. I sat down in my seat, took a deep breath, opened the computer program to enter into the online exam, and started to read the exam question. I read the first paragraph, second paragraph, third paragraph, and what felt like endless paragraphs of this sole question. When I finally finished reading the question, I had no idea how to answer it. I had to keep myself from laughing out loud at what a joke this was. Lawyers are trained at "issue spotting". We are supposed to know how to read or listen to a set of facts and "spot" the potential issues. I couldn't spot any issues in this set of facts. I knew they were there, but I couldn't see them. Four hours later, I uploaded my exam answer and fled the room.

A month or so after winter break, I received my results from the first semester exams. I did well in all of my classes, except Civil Procedure. In Civil Procedure, I received a marginal pass. A marginal pass is the equivalent of a D at my law school (we didn't use the traditional A through F grading system, which was one of the reasons I wanted to come to this school. Honestly, the evaluation system is so much more painful than the traditional grading system when you basically fail an exam!) For someone who received As and Bs my whole life, I couldn't believe what was happening and was devastated. In addition to the marginal pass, the evaluation included a narrative with comments about how my "analysis was insufficient." This narrative became part of my evaluation for my first semester of law school and put a "deficiency mark" on my academic record. This "deficiency mark" meant two things: 1) I had to attend a "remedial class" for the remainder of the second semester in addition to my other classes and 2) if I got another marginal pass, I would be put on academic probation.

I was ticked off. At first at the institution and my professor and the way that I felt like the evaluation characterized me. And then ticked off at myself for giving up on Civil Procedure.

I was standing on the corner of Reed Street and Northampton Street, where my church was located, reading my evaluation, ticked off, and crying to my dad on the phone. It was a Friday night and I was supposed to go into church to help serve with middle schoolers. Yet, there I stood stuck and crying on the street corner feeling as though my insufficient analysis made me insufficient, deficient, and marginal.

Papa didn't allow me to say too many words about these feelings - he knew better and reminded me that I knew better. He encouraged me. He guided me back to my authentic self by reminding me that I couldn't be immobilized by wavering feelings. He reminded me that my legal career wasn't over, that this evaluation didn't define me, and that God hadn't brought me this far to let me fail. Papa heard and understood my emotions. He empowered me to take a step forward by reminding me that I had a commitment to go serve the Lord and those middle schoolers. That was the end of the conversation. I walked into church and moved forward.

Our core values move us. Core values overcome our wavering feelings by whispering truths to us. They are our compass - the north, south, east, and west - that give us clarity. They provide direction that empowers us to live with intention. Living with intention creates space for us to speak intentionally. But in order to clearly see the direction of our guiding principles we have to slow down and dig deeply into our experiences to uncover why we are struck by our experiences.

When I really slow down and dig deeply into my experience of getting a marginal pass, what ticked me off was allowing the words in my evaluation to define and direct me and not my core values. My conversation with my dad struck my internal tuning fork, because even in the brevity of the conversation, he guided me back to clarity of myself. I felt struck by my guiding principles that gave me the freedom to move forward and not stay stuck.

Let me show you how slowing down and dig deeply into our experiences can help you clarify your core values and as a result, your voice. (I like to call this writing in the margins of my own life - a practice that has consistently helped me find and clarify my voice.)

I stood there with my tears and fears and Papa listened, and I mean really listened, to me. He heard what I was saying, reserving judgment and interruption so as to not minimize the importance of my voice. He never pushed aside the very real deep emotions I experienced; I am cursed and blessed with feeling everything very deeply. And on that street corner, I knew he respected my voice and my feelings. This mutuality of respect and never minimizing anyone served as one of the core values in our home. In that brief call, creating a space for mutual respect, struck my tuning fork. When someone can create that kind of space, they can simultaneously support you and encourage you to make a move. That's what Papa did. So, when he suggested a game plan for me to go into the building to follow-through on my commitment, I respected him, because he respected me and empowered me to respect myself and move.

When I make a commitment to something or someone, I am wholly devoted. Devotion is a sacred covenant for me and my dad knew the sacredness of my commitments. In just a few words, he reminded me of my commitment for the evening - a commitment to serve God and His middle schoolers. By shifting my focus to my devotion instead of my devastation, Papa struck my core value of devotion and that guided my steps into the building and into my commitment.

Our short conversation was both a deposit and exchange of wisdom. In fact, I often come back to this story as an archetype for what to do when I'm stuck between my feelings and my commitments. Papa helped me discern how to seize this moment in a way that stewarded my calling well. (You'll remember from the Pink Polka Dot Bean Bag story that the pursuit of wisdom holds a guiding place in my life. I'll also note, that the "Carpe Diem" scene struck me, because of the wisdom unlocked in what Williams tells his students.) I value the wisdom to make decisions with clarity and conviction and to seize the moments in front of us. Standing on that corner crying, I was stuck because I was misaligned with my core values. But my dad knew inside of me I had the wisdom to make a decision with clarity and conviction. I had the wisdom to seize this moment and not be seized by the moment. So, he stood alongside me to guide me towards the wisdom he and I both knew were inside me.

In the midst of my devastation, Papa knew I could take a step forward if he reminded me of my faith. "God didn't bring you this far to let you fail." Faith embraces the unknown in right response to His love, promises, and calling. Faith takes steps through the devastation towards the voice of the One calling for movement. Faith takes steps, even if they are baby steps. My doubt and insecurity, left me paralyzed on that street corner. Paralysis is the opposite of faith; faith moves towards the place that God reveals on the way.

Papa wasn't standing there on the corner with me. He was hundreds of miles away in our home in Florida in his brown rocking chair watching the Nightly News on mute. But love moves. And because love moves, when we are struck by love, we move towards our self and others in love. Papa's love prompted him to move towards me, which prompted me to move towards myself. He sent a love vibration through me to love my God and myself more than my marginal pass. To move towards the image I was created in and to be the God-designed version of myself. And to move in love towards others. That's the beautiful thing about love: When love is activated the ripple effects are unstoppable. When we got off the phone, my internalized feelings that tried to stop me were overcome by a love that made me unstoppable.

Respect, devotion, wisdom, faith, and love were the guiding principles that struck me and caused me to move through my marginal pass and into my authentic God-design. Over the years, as I have walked through experiences, these core values continue to help me move towards myself. They cause me to realign my voice into its most authentic color. This is the power of exploring our core values and exploring them in light of our experiences. Especially exploring them in the challenging experiences that make us feel stuck. When we feel most stuck, the guiding principles support movement. We move, because we remember what's non-negotiable and those non-negotiables become our guides.

Let's jump back into Caleb's story to explore the core values that undergirded his response as he enters the scene of history. Caleb doesn't come out and say: "My core values are XYZ." But we can dig deeply into his story to write in the margins of what made him tick and what ticked him off and why. From the beginning, even before Caleb says a word, we see that Moses chose him as one of the chief leaders to go explore the Promised Land. Now, you don't become a chief leader of a tribe by accident. Especially, a chief leader over the tribe of Judah, the largest and most powerful tribe. By observing Caleb's role in the tribe, we uncover that at a minimum something that made Caleb tick was leading others with courage. In fact one of things that Moses tells the chief leaders is that they ought to "be of good courage" when they went into the land. I wonder if Moses said that knowing that courage would strike the tuning fork inside these men. Caleb seems to speak and move from a place of courage in the beginning of his story and as we'll continue to see throughout his story.

As the story continued, the explorers bring a report of the Promised Land that starts off as favorable, but ends fearful. When Caleb hears the fears, he interrupts the report, quiets everyone, and encourages them to go up and occupy the land, because they were able to overcome it! Let's acknowledge the boldness of Caleb for a moment - we'll see him continue to use his voice in powerful ways. When Caleb interrupts the majority voices, he spoke up because something struck His tuning fork. He was so struck by the fears, that he interrupts the scene to speak against the faithlessness and fearfulness of the ten leaders. Somewhere deep inside of Caleb, he was unwilling to concede defeat, because he was led by a deep conviction that he and the Israelites were overcomers.

Unfortunately, Caleb's dissenting voice did not convince the Israelites of their potential. They complained about their leaders, Moses and Aaron, and begged for new leadership. This strikes Caleb (and Joshua, who was also a minority voice in the story) so deeply that he ends up tearing his clothes in sadness and frustration. In this culture, when someone tore their clothes it was a sign of mourning. Now, I don't know about you, but I don't tear my clothes in mourning every time someone disagrees with my minority opinion. But I do resonate with experiences where I had a clear sense of what God was calling me to do and people dismissed my voice. Caleb had a clear sense of what God was calling them to and he spoke from a place of unwavering integrity to that truth, but the people didn't support or agree with him. In fact, they questioned his integrity. Caleb - as we'll continue to see - is a man of incredible integrity and that integrity strikes and moves him through his experiences.

Caleb came up against what seemed like insurmountable odds that may have kept others silent. But his external reality did not match the guiding principles inside of him. His core values caused him to not stay silent. He spoke from a voice that was found in a Spirit-filtered mentality and he was led by what struck his internal tuning fork.

Color You _____ Moment

As we adventure together on the journey to find our voices in the tension between God's promises and their fulfillment, I want to empower you through "Color You _____ Moments". I alluded to this in Chapter One, but now that we're officially coming into our first Moment, I want to explain the intention of these Moments.

"Color You _____ Moments" will include questions and coloring exercises to help you discover your color. This process takes time, but I guarantee the journey will transform you into the God-designed version of yourself. These questions and exercises are ones that I've done myself and I've guided folks of all ages and backgrounds through to support them in finding their voice. Writing in the margins of your life is powerful. It's a way to respond and react to what God is saying to your soul. Don't allow this to be a monologue where God talks at you; allow this to be a dialogue where you and God have a conversation about your color. It's in those spaces of dialogue where you will find your voice - your color to add to God's masterpiece. So, take out a journal and let's slow down, dig deep, and make moves!

Questions to Ponder:
- Think back over the past several weeks. Write about an experience that made you tick or ticked you off.
- Reflect on why this experience made you tick or ticked you off by asking yourself:
  - What were the emotions I felt?
  - What were the responses I gave?
  - What were the reactions I had afterwards?

Coloring Exercise: Values Cards
- Grab 40 index cards and write the following words on them (36 of the cards will have a word on them and 4 will be left blank in case you want to add your own words - which I encourage you to do. Remix and remake this in a way that honors your tuning fork!):
  - Wealth
  - Wisdom
  - Power
  - Freedom
  - Trustworthiness
  - Accountability
  - Knowledge
  - Success
  - Professionalism
  - Integrity

- Justice
- Dedication
- Respect
- Humor
- Helpfulness
- Love
- Independence
- Loyalty
- Faith
- Health
- Security
- Responsibility
- Morality
- Religion
- Recognition
- Life
- Cooperation
- Compassion
- Honesty
- Patience
- Work
- Advancement
- Spirituality
- Empathy
- Beauty
- Creativity

- Spread all 40 index cards out word-side up
- Flip over the index cards that don't resonate with you until you've narrowed it down to five.
    - (Generally, people can narrow it down to within 10 and then begin to struggle. Something that may help you to narrow it down is to explore definitions of the words you've chosen so far. To be honest, I actually have a top six list of core values, because I couldn't narrow it down to five.)
- Once you've chosen your top five (or six), continue to explore definitions in order to write your own explanation for each of your core values
- Look back at the experience you wrote that made you tick or ticked you off. Write the core values you see striking you in that story

CORRECTIVE LENSES

"It's not how hard you hit, it's how hard you can get hit and keep moving forward. That's how winning is done." Rocky Balboa

This was the first chapter I wrote in this book. It's also the last chapter I wrote. The first time I wrote this chapter was in February 2015 - two months after my father passed away. My friends sent me away to Montpelier, Vermont for a weekend, so that I could be alone and process the incredible loss that I'd just experienced. During that weekend, I wrote. I wrote a chapter about perspectives and how to see our experiences through the lens of faith. I didn't think the words that I wrote would be the beginnings of a book. I wrote as a healing exercise. I wrote as an attempt to work through some of my initial emotions and feelings. I wrote to stir my own faith as I wrestled in the tension of a loss that I could not fully comprehend. I wrote about perspectives, because I felt like I was in a fog and couldn't see. I wrote to find my voice - my yellow - again.

And then in 2016 when I embarked on the journey of writing this book, I included that chapter, because it felt like such an important part of finding your voice in the tension between God's promises and their fulfillment. Even though it felt like such an important part, it went through a series of edits and revisions. The idea of our perspectives evolved to thinking about our mindset and how our mindset encompasses the perspectives that impact our reactions and response to our experiences.

With all of the edits and revisions, you'd think that it would've finally landed in a place that felt complete. But as I made my way through the editing process (in February 2018, three years after I wrote the initial chapter), something was still missing. So, I scrapped it. I decided I need to write it again from scratch. The concepts were there, but my voice wasn't clear. My voice sounded foggy - just like I felt when I wrote it.

You may be wondering at this point - okay why are you telling me all of this? I share this, because finding our voice is a process. In the three year journey of writing this book, I've been forced to hone my voice to ensure these words clearly communicate ideas that can support you in finding your voice. And as we embark on this journey, we move through the fog to uncover clarity. Clarity of our mindset gives us clarity for how to react and respond to our experiences. If, together, we can find clarity in our mindset, then we can learn to speak our God-designed color into our experiences.

Mindset: Perspectives that impact how you react and respond to your experiences

How Do You See?

I've been wearing glasses since tenth grade. In fact, I got glasses and braces within a few weeks of each other. This was long before wearing glasses was cool. So, I was doubly not cool! By the time I got to college, I traded in my glasses for contacts. Then, during my senior year, glasses became cool. I bought a new pair of glasses. Plus, I was going to law school and I wanted to have that smart lawyer look. A few years later, Warby Parker changed everything and now are you even cool if you don't wear glasses?

Coolness aside, without my glasses, everything is blurry. I can see that people, cars, and trees are there, but I need corrective lenses to see clearly. In the same way, my physical eyes need corrective lenses, my spiritual eyes also need corrective lenses. The corrective lens of faith has transformed my mindset and informs all of my perspectives. Without it, I can't see anything clearly.

How do you see?
Let's take this question a little deeper: How do you see your experiences clearly?

Maybe you're one of those blessed souls with 20/20 vision and the reality of corrective lenses isn't something that connects to your experience. But, all of us have souls and our souls have eyes that need corrective lenses. The inner eye of the Spirit observes our experiences to perceive what's happening and informs how we react and respond to those experiences. Our inner eye needs the corrective lens of faith.

In January of 2008, my senior year of college, I went to Boston and New York to tour law schools (and honestly to see if I could withstand the arctic temperatures of the Northeast). I believe wholeheartedly in going to visit schools before you apply to them. I've learned over and over again, when you're a child of God, your Heavenly Dad goes into these places with you, with a greater perspective then you have, to grow your mindset of what's possible. I'll never forget stepping onto Northeastern's campus and walking into the law school building. I knew instantly that this was the place that God wanted me to attend. He didn't scream it in an audible voice, but I felt it in a gentle whisper in my spirit. Over the next few days, I visited several law schools, but God left this imprint on my perspective about what was possible for me.

As I waited to hear from the schools I'd applied to, I asked God to not let wherever I went only be about going to law school. We talked about how I wanted to make an impact for Him in whatever city we would go to next. I wanted it to be about something more. My experience at Northeastern and my mindset about going to law school there grew so expansive I could visualize my life and opportunities.

But then I started getting rejection letters. I overanalyzed everything. I started thinking too much. I wondered if I'd made a mistake applying to law school. I wondered if I had made up the perspective God whispered to me. I wondered if my mindset was all wrong. My over analysis led to a fear and hopelessness that I wouldn't get into any law school.

One day, that same friend who told me she would "color me yellow" until I believed it sat across from me at our college bookstore. As we drank cinnamon spice lattes and I went on and on about my fears and hopelessness, she asked me: "why are you so eager to get into schools that don't want you?"

I focused on my fear. I focused on my feelings. I focused on myself. Focusing on all of this, caused me to forget my faith. I let myself be controlled by my fears. I took my eyes off of my Father. My feelings became louder than His truths. My mindset became small. I became small. And the truth remained: the law school that did want me hadn't sent out acceptance letters yet. I didn't have to settle for schools that didn't want me.

After she asked that question, I stopped allowing fear to determine how I saw and started to allow faith to frame my perspective about my acceptance into law school. Several weeks later, buried in a stack of mail, a big envelope waited for me from Northeastern with an acceptance letter inside. Next fall, Fall of 2008, I, Sarah Gautier, would be enrolled at Northeastern School of Law in Boston!

In that moment, I remembered the whisper of the Spirit to my soul when I stepped onto Northeastern's campus. I remembered my dream to go to law school that God had planted inside of me at a very young age. I remembered the faithfulness of His promises. I remembered the power of the corrective lens of faith and how seeing through faith has always empowered me to see beyond my fears.

I cannot tell you the amount of times, I've looked at circumstances, just like this experience of getting into law school, and what I see has terrified me. Fear is real. Fear is so real that the bible tells us approximately 365 times not to fear and not to be afraid. This isn't just a simple reminder. This is a word of acknowledgement and encouragement from a Heavenly Father who knows the very real fears of His children. I'm thankful that I'm part of a Kingdom and family, where the One who leads me, doesn't dismiss my very real fears when what I'm looking at does not look like something I can see through. And He doesn't dismiss your fears either.

Remember, Mary, Jesus's mother. She was a teenager who found out she was miraculously pregnant with Jesus, the Messiah, the Savior of the World, the God-man. And we know she was afraid, because when the angel appears to her to break the news of what had happened, the first thing the angel says is "Fear not." Are you kidding me, angel? "Fear not." I'm looking at this circumstance and there's a lot for me to fear here, including but not limited to, how I am going to explain to my fiancé, Joseph, that we're having a baby when we've never had sex. Okay, angel, fear not, okay.

But then the angel explains to her why she can "fear not" saying that she was highly favored by God and the potential of the One who was conceived inside of her was limitless: "For nothing will be impossible with God.[13]" Now, I'm 100% certain that Mary's fears didn't disappear instantly when the angel says these things to her and I'm also 100% certain that Mary was able to look beyond her fears and see through her faith that the potential growing inside of her was greater than the fears in front of her.

The eyes of our souls long to be framed by the corrective lens of faith. "Now faith is the assurance of things hoped for, the conviction of things not seen.[14]" Faith allows us to see with clarity the unseen things that will soon be seen. When we have a mindset of faith, it doesn't mean the fears disappear, it just means the fears aren't the focus that's clouding our clarity. Without faith, our soul's inner eye becomes blinded and our mindset becomes eroded, so that we can no longer see.

What Do You See?

Rewind to when Moses sent the twelve young leaders out to explore the Promised Land and they came back with several reactions and responses to their mission. They all came back affirming how the Promised Land was indeed a land flowing with milk and honey and it was prosperous. However, ten of the young leaders focused on the fortified walls around the cities, the giants from the descendants of Anak, and the strong tribes in the land. They focused on their weaknesses and on their enemies' strengths. Then Caleb responds by quieting everyone and speaking according to his faith. Caleb says: "Let us go up at once and occupy it, for we are well able to overcome it.[15]"

They all saw the same land, but they saw the land differently. Ten of them could not see through their faith beyond their fears. So, their fears eroded their mindset, so that what they saw were obstacles and opposition. They focused on the pitfalls and not God's promises. Even though the Lord already told them the land was theirs, they feared actually possessing the Promised Land. And as a result, they aren't allowed to enter into the Promised Land.

On the other hand, Caleb and Joshua, allowed faith to frame their mindset about the land they saw. They focused on the promises of God, more than the hurdles. Their faith caused them to run towards the promise, not from the promise. The text doesn't tell us this, but we would be oversimplifying this, if we didn't acknowledge that Caleb had fears about possessing the Promised Land. Caleb saw the same obstacles and opposition that the ten young leaders saw. The difference in Caleb was that he saw through the obstacles and opposition to the potential and possibilities. When Caleb interrupts the ten young leaders and says, "we are well able to overcome it," Caleb's mindset relied more on his faith in what God would do than on a fear in what God may not do.

What do you see when you're looking at the circumstances in front of you? This life is a journey full of obstacles and opposition. And when we're seeking to find our voice - our God-designed color, in the tension between God's promises and their fulfillment, the obstacles and oppositions will look like the giants who were on the Promised Land. So, the mindset we bring to uncovering the voice inside of us matters. When our mindset is fixed on fear we don't get very far. Fixating on our fear will cause us to forfeit our future. I will even dare to say that if we can't look passed our fears and see through our faith, we will never find our voice. We can't allow the fear of giants to overshadow the favor of God. A mindset of faith sees the potential and the possibility. To allow potential and possibility to become our perspective that impacts how we react and respond to our experiences, is to to allow our voice to reveal its color.

We hear Caleb's words revealing how his mindset was framed by faith: "Let us go up at once and occupy it, for we are well able to overcome it.[16]" These are the first words we ever hear come out of Caleb's mouth. These are first sounds of his voice. These are first strokes of his color on the canvas of history. "We are well able to overcome it." I'm not convinced that if I were in Caleb's shoes, I would be the one with these epic first words. In fact, part of me wonders if I would be hanging out with the ten young leaders saying: "Nah nah nah, I'm a 'grasshopper[17]' compared to those giants, I'm not going into that land."

When we have a mindset that sees the potential, our voices create space for the possibilities. Wearing the corrective lenses of faith, brings our perspectives into alignment with our potential. When God designed us, He designed us with extraordinary potential. And not only designed us with potential, but invites us to collaborate with Him in continuing to steward creation and create new things. God is faithful to fulfill His promises as we are faithful to see and speak according to our potential. Our voice ought to speak like Caleb's voice did. Caleb spoke according to his potential and because he spoke according to his potential, he enlarged to the space of his potential. When we speak from a mindset of faith, we grow into our potential and we begin to possess the extraordinary inside of us.

Let's allow faith to empower us to speak beyond our fears and into the promises that have been secured for us. Let's not allow fear to make us small. Speaking out of our fear traps us into a box. And it traps God into a box. Let us not limit what God wants to do in and through us, because our foggy, blurry, undefined voice is too afraid to speak the possibilities into existence. Let's not live small lives. Our fears can trap our lives. Let's live in the fullness of our faith. Let's live lives that are large, because our inner eye is framed by a mindset that sees through our faith passed our fears and speaks possibilities into realities.

(Fun fact: I rewrote this chapter in one sitting and I wrote it with my glasses off, so that I can experience just how important corrective lenses are for my physical eyes and for my spiritual eyes.)

Color You _____ Moment

Questions to Ponder:

- Think about a challenging experience you've had in the past year. When you were in that experience, how did you see that what was happening?

Coloring Exercise: Setting Intentions

"Finally, brothers (and sisters), whatever is true, whatever is honorable, what is pure, whatever is lovely, whatever is commendable, if there is any excellence, if there is anything worthy of praise, think about these things." [Philippians 4:8]

One of the most important practices that I've learned in the journey of finding my voice is framing my day with intentions. Throughout our days, we can experience countless experiences that can impact us. But when we set intentions, we set our mindset.

This verse is a good place to start to set intentions. Here are two options for ways that you can use this verse to help you set intentions and set your mindset.

Option 1: Choose one phrase (whatever is true, whatever is honorable, etc) for the week
Option 2: Focus on one phrase for each day of the week

Before you start your day, reflect and visualize:
-    What will it mean to set my mind on that particular phrase?
-    How will I allow that phrase to frame how I react and respond to my experiences?

Before you end your day, reflect and visualize: what did it mean to set my mind on that particular phrase and how did that phrase frame how I reacted and responded to my experiences.

LOOK OUT TO SEE

"Sometimes who we are, just like the dreams we have, and the love we're building, needs to be called into existence before it can grow. Sometimes saying, 'I'm a writer,' is the first step." // Ally Fallon, Packing Light

The bar exam. The haunting rite of passage after law school graduation. After three years in law school, this final step stood between me and practicing law. I had about two months to study the summer after graduation. I spent half of every day at a coffee shop watching roughly three hours of lecture videos on topics from property law to constitutional law. The other half of every day, I spent rewriting my notes, practicing multiple choice questions, and writing essays. I studied. I studied hard.

Finally, the end of July arrived. When I applied to take the bar exam, I requested to take it in western Massachusetts. Taking the bar exam in the convention center in Boston with hundreds of Type-A law students with their anxious energy bouncing off the walls of the room seemed like a level of Dante's inferno to me, so I opted for the calmer and smaller atmosphere at the site in western Massachusetts. I reserved a room at a hotel close to the testing site and arrived the day before the exam. I committed to resting my brain that day. Whatever I didn't know by now definitely would not magically get engraved in my brain at this point.

I woke up the day of the bar exam, showered, ate breakfast, took my time, and spent the whole morning praying. I repeated words my parents told me: "God didn't bring you this far to leave you here." "Do your best and God will do the rest." I drove in silence to the testing site and waited for the exam proctors to let us into the room. I sat down in my seat.

God, please don't let me have a frantic eraser person next to me who will shake the table. God, give me a forcefield of grace and supernatural knowledge. God, bring to my mind everything that I studied and learned throughout the past few weeks and help the right facts in the fact patterns to jump off the page to me. Let's do this!

Two days of taking the bar exam. Eight hours each day. Pure exhaustion. The bar exam is as much a mental feat as a physical feat. After it was over, I slept. The kind of sleep you sleep after pulling an all-nighter. I slept. And then I went on vacation to San Francisco with my parents. People like to call these vacations a "bar trip." I didn't realize until I took the bar exam how much you actually DO need a "bar trip" on the other side of the exam.

The results for the bar exam come out in Massachusetts around Halloween, so I started my two new part-time jobs when I returned from San Francisco. The week before graduation, I received a call from my supervisor for one of my law school co-ops and she asked if I would like to do a post-graduate fellowship at the organization. She was going on maternity leave and they needed someone to lead the project in her absence. However, the position was part-time and I knew that I needed more than a part-time salary to stay in Boston. I set up a meeting with my supervising pastor at church and asked about the possibility of the church bringing me on as a part-time youth pastor. God made miraculous doors open for me and in September after taking the bar exam, I started as part-time youth pastor and part-time "lawyer."

I admittedly felt the pressure and expectations of juggling two part-time jobs that required full-time hours. With the bar exam in the back of my mind, I dug my heels into giving my best to these jobs. Meanwhile, in the beginning of October, I attended the Catalyst Conference in Atlanta with some friends from church. I'd never been to a conference of this magnitude, but from the first session to the last I was blown away by the inspiration of it all.

Judah Smith took the stage and at the time I hadn't heard of Judah, so I didn't have any expectations of the message he would share. From the start of his sermon, I loved his humor and his quirkiness. I loved that he was so rooted in the text and accessible at the same time - my kind of preaching! He spoke about Moses seeing the glory of God[18] and how we experience a greater degree of glory because Jesus has turned towards us.[19]

Judah came to the end of his sermon. I felt something shift in his spirit. The conclusion seemed different than what he planned. He spoke what felt like a prophetic word to young leaders. He shared that so many of us felt the pressure and expectations for the roles given to us to steward. He then read about the sufficiency of God's grace: "My grace is sufficient for you, for my power is made perfect in weakness.[20]" He closed his sermon with these words: "Jesus is enough."

I have read and heard these words hundreds of times, but this time it was different. Jesus is enough. The weight of God's sufficiency. The glory of His grace and His power weighed so heavily on me. As everyone rose to stand, I stayed seated. I sat there weeping in awe of the magnitude of God and yet His mindfulness of the details of my life. I didn't know in that moment that the sufficiency of God's grace and of God's power made perfect in my weakness would incarnate into a principle I would need to get through the next year and a half.

Halloween came. The letter from the Board of Bar Examiners came. I didn't pass. I failed.

My adrenaline stopped. My heart rate slowed down. My thoughts stopped. Glued to my couch the rest of the day, I went numb.

God, I studied so hard for this. God, I thought we had this. This was the vision? What happened? What did I do wrong? How did I mess this up? I'm a failure. I'm a failure.

So many people were waiting to hear how I did. I had to share the news. "Don't worry. You'll try again in February." "It's okay, this test doesn't define you." "You did your best." But really what do all of you know!?! Leave me alone.

I registered again to take the exam in February. In the midst of studying for the second bar exam, I had to fly home to Florida, because my grandfather was in the hospital. We knew he didn't have much time left. I returned to Boston a few days before he passed away and a couple weeks before the bar exam. I studied. I studied hard. Distraught and defeated. Grieving and sad. I pushed through the pain and disillusionment to take the bar exam again. Back at the same hotel in western Massachusetts. I woke up the day of my second bar exam, showered, ate breakfast, took my time, and spent the whole morning praying. I repeated words my parents told me: "God didn't bring you this far to leave you here." "Do your best and God will do the rest."

Another attempt. And a couple of months later, another defeat. I failed again.

This was supposed to go very differently. I was supposed to pass. That was the vision. What happened to "God didn't bring you this far to leave you here." "Do your best and God will do the rest." I'd been left. I'm not good enough. I'm a failure. What happened to the vision? We were supposed to finish law school, pass the bar exam, and become a lawyer. God that was the plan. You brought me this far to pass, not to fail.

And then a good friend of mine told me that I may not be a lawyer by the laws of the state, but I was already a lawyer in the eyes of the Kingdom of God. In my role as youth pastor, I defended the lives of young people before the presence of God. I was so stuck in my own defeat, that I'd lost sight of the sufficiency of God's power made perfect in my weakness. I was a lawyer in the eyes of the Kingdom. And not only in my role as a youth pastor, but in my legal work, I was practicing law without being an official lawyer. I hadn't been left. I was good enough. I wasn't a failure. I registered to take the bar exam for a third time.

This third time, I told God this wasn't negotiable - we were passing. I wasn't taking this bar exam another time after this time. So, this had to be the time for the fulfillment of His promise. I wasn't taking no for an answer. I studied. I studied hard. This time I took two weeks off of work and church. I hid myself completely from everything to focus on nothing, but studying.

For the third time, I returned to the hotel in western Massachusetts. I woke up the day of my third bar exam, showered, ate breakfast, took my time, and spent the whole morning praying. I repeated words my parents told me: "God didn't bring you this far to leave you here." "Do your best and God will do the rest." Another attempt.

Halloween came. The letter from the Board of Bar Examiners came. I passed.

You know that feeling…the feeling of when you come up from the water after trying to hold breath for as along as you can. You come up, break through the water line, and you breathe the biggest gulp of air you can inhale. That. That's how I felt. This wasn't a sigh of relief, this was an exhalation of life!

The dream of a three-year-old little girl to become a judge sparked by watching Nightcourt. The dream that led to a vision to become an attorney and directed my goals through middle school, high school, and college. The promise that "God didn't bring you this far to leave you here" and "Do your best and God will do the rest." Now staring at me in the form of a one-page letter, the vision had all become a reality.

> **Vision:** *God's perspective about you that you may not see yet, but is who you were always meant to be.*

In the tension, we face the compelling temptation to lose complete sight of the long-term vision and sell out to the short-term losses. Once we've sold out to the short-term losses, we quickly find ourselves becoming who we were never meant to be. But God's deep desire for us is to become who we were always meant to be even in the tension when we can't see clearly. Vision causes us to make the shift towards God's perspective about us, to clarify and verify His vision over and over, and to lean into and live out our God-design.

The Land Flowing With Milk and Honey

Moses understood vision and as a mentor to the twelve young leaders, he likely did his best to instill vision into them. I imagine Moses understood the importance of vision and visionary leadership, because of the encounter he had with God when God called him to lead the people out of slavery in Egypt into the Promised Land. In Exodus 3, we read about the famous burning bush encounter between God and Moses. Here, God tells Moses about the Promised Land - the "land flowing with milk and honey.[21]" God saw the affliction and enslavement of His people in Egypt and God saw the land He promised to Abraham and his descendants hundreds of years earlier. God knew this generation who lived in those conditions needed more than just the words of the promise, they needed a picture of the vision. So God uses this proverbial phrase - "a land flowing with milk and honey" - to describe the abundance and fertility of the land He would bring them into through Moses's leadership.

Moses and the Israelites find themselves at the edge of the vision and seeing all the possibilities. He instructs them to bring back some of the fruits from the land. Now, they would not only hear about the Promised Land, but they would experience the vision firsthand. They had an extraordinary opportunity to taste and see God's perspectives in the land He'd already promised belonged to them. I can imagine the twelve young leaders going into the land and tasting the abundance and fertility of the Promised Land. What an opportunity for a generation born into the slavery of Egypt to make the shift away from who they'd always been to who they were meant to be. What a way to clarify and verify vision. What an experience to practice leaning into and living out their God design.

When the twelve young leaders return, all of them experienced God's reality for them. All of them come back saying the land was indeed a "land flowing with milk and honey." They knew the vision and experienced the reality of it. They even brought back fruit from the land to share with the other Israelites. But something in ten of the young leaders stopped them from courageously heading towards the vision. We know they lacked clear values and had static fearful mindset that contributed to stopping them, but there's a third piece that stopped them from pursuing the promise: They didn't make the shift. They didn't shift their gaze to God's perspective about them, even though they saw the land.

As a result of not making the shift to God's perspective about them, they couldn't clarify and verify the vision. Instead they caused confusion in the Israelites about why God brought them into the desert. They caused confusion about Moses as their leader. They even attempted to convince the Israelites to return to the slavery in Egypt that God Himself had rescued them from in order to flee the fear of possessing the promise.

However, Caleb had a "different spirit". Caleb and Joshua made the shift to gaze towards God's perspective about them. The visionary leadership of Moses and their experience in the Promised Land enabled them to make the shift to see this land flowing with milk and honey. Caleb and Joshua attempted to compel the people to make the shift by clarifying and verifying the land was "exceedingly good." They leaned into and lived out their God-design and attempted to compel others to lean into and live it out as well.

But the people were too afraid. This spirit of vision inside of Caleb and Joshua caused them to receive the blessing of being the only two from that generation allowed to enter into the Promised Land.

Make the Shift

What went wrong? The Israelites didn't make the shift to God's perspective about them. This is also the crucial piece that tends to go wrong for all of us. On the journey of finding our voice, we tend to falsely believe that our voice is found separate from God. We don't create our voice, we find our voice. Our voice is a gift we receive as we uncover the color we were designed to paint on the masterpiece of life. We cannot make the false mistake of focusing so much on ourselves that we lose sight of our Creator. When we are in communion with God, we uncover His perspective about us and the voice deep inside of us. Vision separate from God's perspective about us, isn't sustainable vision. We may get a fleeting opportunity to taste and see the vision for a moment like the ten young leaders did. However, vision found in our perspective about ourselves won't give us the opportunity to savor and enjoy God's vision for us for eternity.

What do we get wrong?

During my senior year of college, I took an elective class called "The Book of Job - As Literature." It was a philosophy class and the content intrigued me. We had one assignment for the class - write a critical literary analysis paper.

As an English Literature major, this type of assignment fell squarely into my wheelhouse. Throughout my coursework, I'd developed an interest in identity construction and development in literature. Nearly all of my theses for research papers had an identity slant to them. "The Book of Job - As Literature" was no different. My basic premise was that even though everything was taken away from a just man like Job[22], his identity was not based on his just-ness, but on God's justice. I wrote about how our vision of what is just does not determine how God administers His justice.

And it's precisely because Job's identity was not rooted in his just-ness, that in the end he's able to say "I know my Redeemer lives.[23]" Job made the shift. He shifted his vision of himself towards God's vision of him - someone deeply loved by God no matter what the circumstances looked like to Job.

If Job had not made the shift, he would have mistakenly believed - like His friends tried to convince him - that he did something that deserved punishment. But God's perspective about us isn't based on our deserving His love and promises or not deserving them. Our present state does not dictate His perpetual promises. Our just-ness, goodness, badness, evilness, or any other "-ness" does not motivate God to want to bring us into our Promised Lands. God is motivated by the affection He set on us when He chose to create us.

When Moses prepares the people to enter into the Promised Land he tells them:

> "For you are a people holy to the Lord your God. The Lord your God has chosen you to be a people for his treasured possession, out of all the peoples who are on the face of the earth. It was not because you were more in number than any other people that the Lord set his love on you and chose you, for you were the fewest of all peoples, but it is because the Lord loves you and is keeping the oath that he swore to your fathers that the Lord has brought you out with a mighty hand and redeemed you from the house of slavery, from the hand of Pharaoh king of Egypt. Know therefore that the Lord your God is God, the faithful God who keep His covenant and steadfast love with

those who love him and keep his commandments,
to a thousand generations." [Deuteronomy 7:6-9]

God is motivated by the love He set on us. We get it wrong
when we think His perspective about us is conditional on us.
Moses teaches us that God's perspective of us is that we are holy,
chosen, and His treasured possession. Since we are holy from
God's perspective, He already sees us as not a common people,
but as a people who are set apart to Him. And not simply that
we are set apart to Him, but chosen among all people and called
His. Perhaps the most beautiful reality of God's perspective of
us is that we are God's treasured possession. As God's treasured
possession, we have been personally acquired by Him and we
are carefully preserved in Him. Like a special work of art, God
chooses us and preserves us with His love towards us. His love
is set on us, not because of our just-ness, goodness, badness, or
evilness. His love is set on us, because His love is as natural as
breathing; it's a love that is essential to who He is.

So when we misunderstand His perspective of us and believe that
it's motivated by us, we get it wrong. He moves in love towards us,
because it's essential to who He is as our God. When He looks
at us He sees us as who He designed us to be and longs to bring
us into that vision. His desire to bring us into His perspective is
not conditional on where we are now. It's conditional on who He
has always been.

Why is it crucial?

You are a finite creation with infinite potential. Inside of you is
the potential to enter into the vision God has for you. Inside of
you is the potential to uncover your eternal purpose. Inside of
you is the potential to find your God-design. We ought to spend
time on the journey to find ourselves, to find our identity, and

to find our voice. Making the shift to God's perspective of us is a journey of uncovering what lies deep within us - a truth that's woven into our core.

Jesus shares this reality with his followers:

> "Whoever finds his life will lose it, and whoever loses his life for my sake will find it." [Matthew 10:39]

As we make the shift to God's perspective, we'll be found within our infinite potential. Finding ourselves in our infinite potential will cost all the temporal things, but we will gain every eternal thing. It's crucial that we train our finite minds to think in terms of infinite. God's visions cannot be fulfilled with a sprint-mentality focused on our ability to run fast for a short term. Making the shift towards God's perspective means adopting a marathon-mentality where we can go harder for longer. God doesn't want us to be in this race for the sprints of our finite. God wants us to be in this race for the marathon of His infinite.

Shifting Our Perspective

We can get it right. Making the shift from our perspective about ourselves to God's perspective about us is a shift we can make.

We make the shift by counting the cost.

Making the shift to follow the vision of God will cost us temporary things, but it grants us every eternal thing. The invitation to make the shift towards God's perspective comes at a cost. Every shift comes with a cost. Every decision comes with a cost. Every time we commit to one thing, it comes at the expense of another thing.

"For which of you, desiring to build a tower, does not first sit down and count the cost, whether he has enough to complete it? Otherwise, when he has laid a foundation and is not able to finish, all who see it begin to mock him, saying, 'This man began to build and was not able to finish.'" [Luke 14:28-30]

If we long to pursue the vision that God has given us, then we are pursuing an eternal building project that comes. If we desire to live a life with the core of who we are pointed towards God's vision for us, then we're guaranteed there will be a cost.

What will the vision God has given you cost you?

We make the shift by surrendering.

In high school, I went snorkeling in Puerto Rico. I was excited for the adventure. I have always been a bit of an adventure junky. I couldn't wait for the experience of seeing the world beneath the surface of the sea. My cousins and I got geared up for the adventure - goggles, breathing tubes, flippers, the whole deal - and we set out on a boat into the water. We planned to make three stops along the way. When we came to the first stop, the instructor told us that all we had to do was kick our flippers and float just below the surface of the water and look down. I climbed down the ladder off the side of the boat into the ocean.

I freaked out. I basically had what felt like a panic attack. I couldn't just make myself kick my flippers and float right below the surface of the water and look down. I started kicking, but frantically kicking, so hard that the kicking turned to flailing. My heart started racing. I started feeling extremely hot. I started gasping for air. Get me back in the boat.

When we got to the second drop area the same thing happened. The instructor told me that I just had to trust that the water would carry me. I thought, "I just? Just? Easy for you to say. I just can't do this."

We got to the third drop area and at this point I knew it was a lost cause, so I just sat on the boat watching the water from a safe distance.

This is when I was confronted with my fear: I couldn't relinquish control to the sea. The thought of this powerful force that was greater than me taking control of me - was unfathomable. So instead, I kicked and flailed like a fish out of water.

When I think about surrender, I think about snorkeling. Surrendering to something outside of myself and something more powerful than myself, sends me back into that water - flailing. Being in the tension is not an invitation to be tense. When God declares a promise over us, we don't have to force it into existence. In fact, making the shift to His perspective, is at its core an invitation to surrender. It's about releasing our grip on the promises and living open to the adventure. It's about not getting tense in the tension.

If anyone had a reason to be tense in the tension, it was Jesus just before going to the cross. In the Garden of Gethsemane during his last hours, he kicked and flailed, he sweat blood all while begging God to allow this tension to pass from him. But then, he surrenders. He says to His Dad, your will, Dad, not mine. The tension releases, as the surrender increases. This act of surrender shifts the scene. This release shifts the reality that you and I get to experience. Jesus's surrender secures our salvation. The salvation that we get the choice to accept - the radical love that died on a cross and conquered death, so that we would never have to experience the pain of death. It's a surrender to die to our life and be resurrected into new life with Christ. It's a shift. It's a surrender that grants us citizenship in the Kingdom of God - the place we were ultimately always meant to be.

We make the shift by living by faith.

"Touch the Sky" by Hillsong United just started playing on my Spotify. I couldn't have cued that up better if I tried. The chorus of this song says: "My heart beating, My soul breathing, I found my life when I laid it down, Upward falling, Spirit soaring, I touch the sky, when my knees hit the ground." This is the aftermath of surrender. "Being found" and "falling upward" happens because we are found in the Creator and we learn to live by faith.

Paul, the Apostle, says it this way:

> "I have been crucified with Christ. It is no longer
> I who live, but Christ who lives in me. And the
> life I now live in the flesh I live by faith in the Son
> of God, who loved me and gave himself for me."
> [Galatians 2:20]

The act of surrender crucifies us with Christ and our new life is lived IN Christ. We live in the reality of Christ's resurrection and not in the decay of our death. We live in the faith of His redemptive power that brought us from death to life and that aroused us from sleep to awakening. When we're found in our Creator, we take on not only His life, but also His perspective. The infinite perspective of God's vision operates in us.

We make the shift by fanning into
flame the gift of sincere faith.

Making the shift to God's perspective is not a one-time act. At the end of his life, Paul, the Apostle, writes to Timothy, his mentee and "little brother" who leads the church in Ephesus. The church in Ephesus was growing, but confronting all kinds of false teachings. Paul's last words to Timothy are words of encouragement to continue towards God's vision despite the obstacles.

He writes these passionate words to Timothy:

> "I am reminded of your sincere faith, a faith that dwelt first in your grandmother Lois and your mother Eunice and now, I am sure, dwells in you as well. For this reason I remind you to fan into flame the gift of God, which is in you through the laying on of my hands, for God gave us a spirit not of fear but of power and love and self-control." [2 Timothy 1:5-7]

Paul reminds Timothy of how to keep the shift onto God's vision. He reminds Timothy of the sincere faith passed down to him and in him. Timothy didn't have a "phony dependence" on God's vision for him. Likewise, our sincere faith in God's vision reveals our true dependence on Him. Like Timothy, we must "fan into flame the gift of God" that's inside of us. Our sincere faith in God's vision is a gift to us. It's a gift that we are called to keep sparked. When we don't keep the spark of faith burning, we fall into the fears that God's vision will never become a reality. But we are explicitly told that we were not given a spirit of fear. Paul didn't want Timothy to be afraid of the vision that God has promised him. Moses didn't want the twelve young leaders to be afraid of the vision that God promised them. God doesn't want you to be afraid of the vision that He has promised you. We have a spirit of power, of love, and of self-control. Making the shift to God's vision means keeping our faith in the vision burning, because the spirit inside of us IS bringing us into our Promised Land.

Clarify and Verify

Finding our voices in His vision also invites us to clarify and verify the vision. God's perspective about our God-design often feels very far away from the current version we see in ourselves. Caleb understood this. Caleb was born into slavery and lived through a desert experience. He had no reason to stand firm in faith of God's perspective about him and his fellow Israelites. In the beginning of his story, we see that his fellow Israelites (also born into and living through the same experience) had no faith in the vision. But Caleb had a "different spirit." In the midst of his reality, he clarified and verified the vision over and over again to confirm the truth of God's perspective about him and his fellow Israelites. This act of clarifying and verifying the vision sets Caleb apart. This act allows Caleb to fully enter into the vision. This act propels Caleb into finding his voice in the tension between God's promises and their fulfillment.

How do you clarify a vision?

Clarifying a vision doesn't happen overnight. God gave Moses the vision of bringing the people of Israel into the land flowing with milk and honey years before Caleb enters the story. And yet, during all those years after God gave the vision, Caleb still stands firmly in God's perspective and promise.

So how do you clarify a vision? God's words on vision to the prophet Habakkuk give us some insight here:

> "I will take my stand at my watchpost and station myself on the tower, and look out to see what he will say to me, and what I will answer concerning my complaint.

And the Lord answered me:

"Write the vision; make it plain on tablets, so he
may run who reads it." [Habakkuk 2:1-2]

Habakkuk, the prophet, lived approximately around the end
of the reign of King Josiah. King Josiah committed to national
revival and rebuilding, despite the imminent threat of Babylonian
captivity. At this time, the kingdom of Israel had long since been
divided into two parts - Israel and Judah - because a civil war tore
the kingdom apart. After this drastic division in the kingdom of
Israel, several kings who reigned in both Israel and Judah turned
their backs on the Lord. Israel had already been overtaken by
its enemies and Judah was next. King Josiah's commitment to
national revival and rebuilding moved the Lord to hold off the
onslaught of captivity, but Habakkuk knew the threat would still
come. The prophet Habakkuk could not understand why God
would stand by idly while their enemies threatened to destroy
them.

In the first chapter, Habakkuk basically asks God: "Are you
kidding me?" If we're honest, we've all had those moments, looking
around at the experience we're living with that nagging question
inside of us towards God, "Are you kidding me?" Habakkuk had
that same question. But what's significant about his story, is after
he's asked the hard and honest questions, we find him going to
action without waiting around for an answer. How often do we
get stuck in our frustration about the chasm between our reality
and our vision that we don't make any moves towards anything?
He takes his stand, stations himself, and looks out to see the vision
God has for this situation.

(Quick side note here before we start to explore how we clarify
a vision. Notice the posture of a visionary. You and I can't see

God's perspective of us, if we don't have the right posture before Him. Make your complaints about your reality. Confront Him. Ask Him why you're facing opposition and obstacles. These are all fair conversations to have with God. In fact, these are exactly the kinds of conversation He's always inviting us to have with Him. But a posture of complaining and blaming won't allow you to truly see the beauty of His perspective of you. Habakkuk's posture paints a better picture. He takes a proactive stand at the watchpost. In ancient times, people were appointed to stand at key places in the walls of a city to watch for what was coming. Habakkuk, though not an appointed watchman takes the posture of a watchman, and stands in the tower to watchfully observe what's to come. He stands on the edge - on the outermost part of his city to discern and clarify what was on the horizon. This is the posture of a visionary. In the midst of the opposition, in the midst of the desert, in the midst of the confusion, a visionary stands at the watch post to patiently see what's coming on the horizon from God. The God who sees and knows all things beyond the horizons.)

Alright, let's jump back into what the Lord tells Habakkuk as he stands in this visionary posture. God gives Habakkuk an action plan for how to clarify a vision. He says 1) write the vision, 2) make it plain, and 3) run with it.

Step 1: Write it down

When you begin to get a glimpse of God's perspective about you, write it down. I cannot tell you how many Moleskine journals I have filled with the glimpses of God's perspective about me and visions He's given about me and my life. To be honest, more than half the time I've written down those perspectives, I've neither seen them in myself at the moment of writing them down nor believed them about myself. And then I look back months and even years later and realized, "okay God, I see you unfolding your visions and promises through me as I become more of who you designed me to be."

When we get those glimpses, even when that vision of us and our lives feels ridiculously far away from where we feel like we are in the moment, writing the vision down is the first step to becoming our God-designed self. If you're someone who regularly attends church, here's an exercise that I tell folks to do at the beginning of my sermons: take notes. Don't allow the sermon to simply be a monologue where God is talking at you, but allow the sermon to become a dialogue where you and God are in a conversation. For some people that means doodling, for others that means outlining, for others that means writing down those key words or phrases that stand out to them, and for others it's a combination of everything. But engaging in a sermon in this way is powerful, because this is one of the many ways that God is trying to give you His perspective about your God-design. Even if you don't attend church regularly, there is not a moment of the day where God is not relentlessly chasing after us to reveal the masterpiece He sees when He looks at us. So, we all have countless opportunities to engage in the dialogue with Him about His vision of us and His promises for us.

Step 2: Make it plain

The beautiful opportunity that happens as a result of writing down the vision is that we get to read and reread it and that brings us into greater clarity. We edit it, we revise it, and we make it plain, until it's a clear vision. For Moses and Caleb the clear vision was that God was going to bring them into the land flowing with milk and honey. This vision was so clear, that it became a proverb for the Israelites. This promise turned into a truth they yearned for and a reality they would eventually behold, despite the fact that it was a vision completely different than their current reality of slavery and the desert. This is what happens when we edit, revise, and make our visions plain: the visions becomes an invitation we can experience.

The Lord takes it a step deeper and tells Habakkuk to "make it plain on tablets." The prophets had a custom where they took the prophetic vision that God gave them and engraved it on boards made of stone, wood, or metal. The imagery of "making it plain on tablets" also carries this ancient Hebrew allusion of the writing on the tablets of our heart. So, here the Lord helps Habakkuk and us to see that clarifying the visions - through writing and editing them - causes them to get dug into the tablets of our hearts. His vision gets dug into that core place of us - our hearts - where our foundations are established.

Step 3: Run with it

The last action step is to run with it. In the verse, we see that the person who reads the written and clarified vision will run with it. And we do not run aimlessly chasing the winds of distraction that can so easily come when we're clarifying the vision God has of us and for us. We run with an aim. We run with intentionality and purpose.

Dreams become visions when we start to run with them. God can give us glimpses of the way He wants to use our colors to paint a masterpiece, but the color can't stay in the imaginary world inside our heads. When the Lord says the person who reads the vision will run with it, He's alluding to the ancient concept of a messenger carrying the tablets containing the vision of reality. The clarified vision we carry inside of us is not a reality we run towards, it's a reality we run with. We take decisive action to run with the reality of the vision now. Every strike of our foot as we run, becomes a place where we leave the mark of our color. As we run with the vision, we become the vision for ourselves and for others. Run with it.

How do you verify a vision?

As we run with the vision, we personalize it. And as we personalize it, we verify the truth and accuracy of the vision.

At the beginning of the story, Moses sends the twelve young leaders into the Promised Land. Moses understood God's heart on vision. God's desire is that we personalize the vision He's given us, so that we can personify that vision. Moses knew that in order for the young leaders to truly verify the vision, they needed to explore it, so they could personally verify its truth. Just like the young leaders, we must also learn to explore the possibilities of our new reality. Moses's instructions placed the twelve young leaders in the midst of God's vision. In the same way, we must place ourselves in the midst of God's vision for us. As we surround ourselves in the vision we can behold what He's planning to do for us and through us. Moses's instructions included a list of questions for the twelve young leaders to answer while they're in the midst of the vision. Moses knew that he needed them to be in the midst of the vision and talk about it.

Imagine for a moment being one of these twelve young leaders. You have a list of questions that Moses asked you to answer about your observations of the vision. You have to describe the vision by talking about the vegetation, the geography, and the fertility of the land that's already yours. Words paint a picture of the reality that you expect. So, when you're in the midst of the vision, it's the talking about it part that gets you excited about it. God wants you to be excited about His vision for you. And that excitement happens when you start living in the midst of your vision and start to talk about all that you observe. This is how you verify that the vision isn't simply an illusion, but a reality that you were God-designed to occupy. Verifying the vision, even before we're in the fullness of it, strengthens us to realize the beauty of the future we will become and behold.

Being in the midst of God's vision, so that we can verify the truth of it, invites us to make space for it. The twelve young leaders were in the Promised Land for 40 days. 40 days, friends. That's almost six weeks. That's 960 hours. And when Moses, chose the twelve people, the Lord told him to send men who were tribal chiefs. These young leaders had responsibilities and influence in their communities. It's not like they were people who had 960 hours of free time. So, this invitation was for people who could commit to making space to be in the midst of the vision. This is a reminder that when God gives us a vision, it's an invitation to make space in our lives to experience what He's showing us in an up-close and personal way.

Also, it's important to note that making space to be in the midst of the vision comes at a cost. The twelve young men were leaders in charge of people, systems, and strategic concerns within their tribes. A 40-day journey to verify God's vision invited them to sacrifice their areas of influence into the hands of God. It invited them to sacrificially give their time to this journey. They had to trust that while they were making space to verify God's vision that God would care for everything back home. The same is true for us. Making space to verify God's vision for us means sacrificing aspects of our lives. It means trusting that while we're making space for His vision, He will tend to the spaces of responsibility and influence.

As we make space, we get to occupy the space of the vision. The twelve young leaders went throughout the whole land and specifically to Hebron. We'll talk more in depth about Hebron later, but let's preview the significance of Hebron. Earlier on in the narrative of Scripture, we come to Hebron as a significant dwelling and resting place for Abraham, Isaac, Jacob, and their families. The historical significance will become tied to Caleb and his descendants as they will eventually settle there as well. Caleb walked through the land that would be his and his descendants. He literally stood in the vision. And not only that, but the text tells us that when they came to the valley outside of Hebron, they cut down a cluster of grapes and carried that vine of grapes on a pole back to the people of Israel. Scholars believe that it took two people to carry the grapes back to the people of Israel and that those two people were Caleb and Joshua. Who knows the accuracy of this theory, but Caleb was part of bringing home the blessing of experiencing the vision because he made space for it. When we make space to verify the vision God has for us, we are blessed to stand in it and to carry the blessing of it.

Even with all of this verifying, ten of the young leaders still didn't get the vision. They looked at the opposition literally standing on God's vision for them and even though they had seen and tasted the vision, they didn't get it. So, they go back to the desert and the people of Israel and basically lose the vision. This happens to us too. We can experience the vision by making space for its reality, but we can still miss the opportunity to fully verify it when we realize we now have to fight for it. We realize that there will be tension. We realize that the vision doesn't just come overnight. We realize that we have to dispossess the opposition to possess the vision. All of this nullifies the vision for us and we perish like the ten young leaders who didn't get it.

Caleb and Joshua realized the fight ahead and the desert ground became their training ground. The desert became an opportunity for them to train themselves for truly fighting for the vision.

Without the desert they wouldn't have been able to possess the promise. This can be our story as well. Ours can be a journey of realizing that verifying the vision is our training ground.

After the Lord tells Habakkuk how to clarify a vision, He lets him know that part of verifying the vision is the delay. God tells him:

> "For still the vision awaits its appointed time;
> it hastens to the end - it will not lie.
> If it seems slow, wait for it;
> it will surely come; it will not delay."
> [Habakkuk 2:3]

Vision waits. It cannot be rushed. Vision cooks slowly like a pot of beans that has soaked overnight and then is finished off with a low flame. Vision takes its time to taste its best. But it will surely come. Caleb and Joshua knew that because they verified the vision in the fight. They knew God had already given it to them and they just needed to fight for it. They knew that if God already promised it, it was the reality they were designed to live. Not a reality given easily, but a reality given adventurously. This is the journey of finding our voice in the vision.

Lean In and Live Out

Caleb made the shift from his perspective about himself to God's perspective of him. He clarified and verified God's vision. These actions empowered Caleb to fight for the vision when the appointed time came. Caleb was one of the two people who demonstrated that he leaned into and lived out the vision. When the ten young leaders realized that they had to fight, they lost sight of God's perspective about them.

God noticed a "different spirit"[24] in Caleb. There was a distinctness about his essence that he leaned into. And because he leaned into his God-design - the very breath of God in him - he also lived out that God-design. He followed the vision fully. There is a God-design in you and it's God's perspective about you. It's the you God designed you to be. It's the you God designed when He breathed His distinct breath into you. And it's that you that He wants you to lean into. If you'll lean into that God-designed you, then you'll live out His vision fully.

After the Lord names Caleb's "different spirit", the vision is personalized for Caleb. The Lord says that Caleb's descendants will "possess" the land. This word in the original Hebrew language means to literally dispossess in order to possess. The fight for God's vision is already won. When we lean into and live out our God-design we will dispossess the opposition to possess the vision. It's a guarantee. It's secure in Him. We're secure in Him. Our voice - found in God's perspective of us - is secure when we lean into and live out our God-design.

"Where there is no vision, the people perish.[25]" This is exactly what we see happen to the ten young leaders in our story. Because they had not found their voice in God's vision, they perished in the desert. But what we see in Caleb - the man with a "different spirit" - is that where there is vision, the people possess. Let's make the journey of finding our voice one that possesses the visions, because we've made the shift to God's vision, we've clarified and verified the vision, and we've leaned into and lived out our God-design.

Color You _____ Moment

Coloring Exercise: Vision Statements

PART 1: Getting Started

We'll start to build your vision statement by answering some questions. Your answers will help identify key components and themes to include in your vision statement.

- What are the things I believe and actively seek to demonstrate in my home, my relationships, my community, my school, my job, etc?
- What purpose(s) do I feel called to fulfill?
- What am I passionate about? What brings me joy?
- How would I live my life if time and resources were not an issue?
- What are my greatest strengths and interests?
- How do I define success, happiness, and/or fulfillment?
- What practices do I need to cultivate in my life?
- What are the obstacles that hold me back? What habits do I need to form to overcome those obstacles?

PART 2: Finding Trends

Organize your responses from Part 1 and your Core Values within one of these parts of your life that we'll call Life Components. Feel free to create other Life Components that resonate with you.

- Family
- Friends
- Spiritual growth and development
- Vocational aspirations
- Health/Wellness
- Other components

PART 3: Writing the Vision

Write no more than 6-7 brief statements. Include statements that address:

- What do I ultimately desire to accomplish in my life?
- Who do I feel called to be?
- What is the legacy I hope to be remembered for?

Think about how you can use information from your past to shape the future. Put the information from each Life Component into one or two action statements.

Write using first person perspective and present tense. For example, under the Health/Wellness Component you would say: "I am separating time to rest, reflect, and recharge through writing and reading" or "I am taking time to exercise consistently and to be mindful about my eating habits."

PART 2

IN THE TENSION

The tension is not an invitation to be tense; the tension is an invitation to be tenacious.

I love to drive, but when I moved to Boston I had to learn how to drive in traffic. I'm talking about the kind of traffic that leaves you trapped in the tunnel for thirty minutes. Traffic that takes you over an hour to go 7 miles. Traffic that's jammed for no good reason. These are the things urban planners ought to think about when they're building roads in cities. They ought to think about how to minimize traffic. And yet, I think they're actually plotting how to maximize traffic and cause road rage! I can predict it. If I plan to drive between 7:30AM and 9:30AM or 3:30PM and 6:30PM in Boston, I will hit traffic.

Maybe you've experienced this urban rush hour nightmare. Here's the reality: you know you will get stuck in the traffic, but you have to get stuck in the traffic to get to where you're headed. You know that even though you're stuck in the traffic, eventually you'll get to the destination. But between our current location and our destination exists the traffic tension.

As drivers, we get to choose our experience in the traffic tension. Do we grip the steering wheel? Do we yell at other drivers? Do we tailgate other cars? Do we remain relaxed, yet alert? Do we demonstrate grace towards other drivers inching into our lane? We choose our experience in the traffic tension.

Just as traffic tension is inevitable, life tension is inevitable. We get to choose our experience in the tension of life. In the tension between God's promises and their fulfillment, we choose to be tense or we choose to be tenacious.

Spoiler alert: God's promises never just happen. We never simply arrive at the destination that God promised us. God promised Caleb that He would possess the land that he saw when he went into the Promised Land. But forty five years would pass before Caleb would possess that land. Forty five years in the tension. Caleb experienced the wilderness years with the Israelites and the transition of leadership from Moses to Joshua. These were intense times for the people of Israel and no doubt intense times for Caleb. Caleb had every reason to be tense in the tension. He had every reason to wonder if the God who promised him the land would actually bring them into the land. But it's in the tension where God prepared him to be the leader who could possess the land God promised him.

We find our voice in the tension, because this is the place where God prepares us to possess His promises. What if we re-envisioned the tension to be the preparation season for the vision? What if instead of the intensity of the tension causing us to be tense, the intensity causes us to be tenacious? What if we embraced the tension as God's way of drawing us nearer to Him and nearer to our God-design?

In the tension, we'll learn about four dimensions of refining our voices. Each of these dimensions give us an opportunity to be tenacious and not tense. These four dimensions build upon the voices we've uncovered and refine our voices to prepare us to be the people who are ready and able to possess the promise at its appointed time. In the tension, frameworks are established, holiness is instilled, wonders are revealed, and war is waged. Let's accept the invitation to be tenacious for the promises of God and cling to our God-design as we refine our voice.

WILDERNESS WANDERINGS

"Once you get into the desert, there's no going back,' said the camel driver, 'And, when you can't go back, you have to worry only about the best way of moving forward. The rest is up to Allah, including the danger.'" // Paulo Coelho, The Alchemist

I'm about to tell you a biblical story you're probably not going to like very much. I didn't like it when I first read it. I didn't understand it. It's one of those stories in the Bible where God does something I couldn't believe. It's one of those stories that made me think: "Come on God, maybe there was another way to deal with this situation??"

But this story is the next and only story during the 38 years of the Israelites' wilderness wanderings. Caleb is not mentioned explicitly, but as a member of the Israelite community he would have seen and experienced these intense few days in the wilderness. If I want to guide us to see the full story of how Caleb found his voice in the tension between God's promises and their fulfillment, I can't leave this part of the story. Even though I can't believe what happens, I water-down our journey, if I skip over what happens in the wilderness of the tension.

I can't edit the wilderness out of my own story. You can't edit the wilderness out of your story. If you've gone through a season that you didn't understand until afterwards, then you can appreciate the disorientation that can come in the wilderness. You can appreciate the mysteriousness of God's ways in the wilderness of the tension. You can appreciate the ways that on the other side of obscurity is an opportunity to see God working. Now, this appreciation does not take away the ways we are challenged in the wilderness. We'll see how the challenges can cause us to resist God in the wilderness, because we don't understand Him. But here's a reminder: God is always motivated by His love for us. Yes, even in the wilderness of the tension. God's affection towards us is why He does what He does and allows what He allows. God's love isn't diminished by our actions and it's not conditional on our behaviors.

It's that motivation of love that frames our wilderness wanderings and frames the wilderness wanderings of the Israelites in this story. If we jumped into this story, without looking at how it fits into the larger story of the Bible, we would miss the framework of God's love. In the verses directly before this story, the Lord reminds the Israelites of His affection and how that affection brought them out of Egypt (another kind of wilderness).[26] The verses that end this story, include a reminder that God's motivation for giving them signs was to preserve their lives, so that they wouldn't die in the wilderness.[27]

Within this framework of God's love for the Israelite community, let's explore this story together.

Under the leadership of Moses and Aaron, the Israelites wandered in circles in the wilderness. They had the opportunity to enter into the Promise Land, but their disbelief led them on a different path towards the promise. During their wilderness wanderings, four men - Korah (a Levite), Dathan, Abiram, and On (three Reubenites) - rallied 250 chief leaders and rose up against Moses and Aaron. They accused Moses and Aaron of going too far by assuming leadership over the community. They claimed everyone was set apart as holy unto the Lord, not just Moses and Aaron. The rebels asked Moses and Aaron: "Why then do you exalt yourselves above the assembly of the Lord?"[28] Essentially, their frustration with Moses and Aaron was "who put you in charge of us?"

These four men incited a rebellion, with a group of Levites as a majority of the people who joined. The Levites were the tribe chosen by the Lord for the priesthood. They were called to be set apart as holy unto the Lord and minister before God in the tabernacle (a movable tent where the presence of the Lord dwelled among the Israelites as they wandered through the desert).

Moses tells Korah and his followers that the Lord would reveal who He chose to lead the Israelites. Moses instructed Korah and his followers that the following day they ought to burn incense before the Lord in boxes called censors. This role was specifically given only to the high priest, as an act set apart as holy to the Lord.[29] When they burned the incense the Lord would reveal the chosen high priest and intercessor for the community.

Then, Moses addresses Korah and the Levites who joined in the rebellion:

> "Hear now, you sons of Levi: is it too small a thing for you that the God of Israel has separated you from the congregation of Israel, to bring you near to himself, to do service in the tabernacle of the Lord and to stand before the congregation to minister to them, and that he has brought you near him, and all your brothers the sons of Levi

with you? And you seek the priesthood also? Therefore, it is against the Lord that you and all your company have gathered together. What is Aaron that you grumble against him?" [Numbers 16:8-11]

Moses attempts to quell the rebellion by asking to speak with Nathan and Abiram. But they refuse to meet with Moses, saying:

"Is it a small thing that you have brought us up out of a land flowing with milk and honey, to kill us in the wilderness, that you must also make yourself a prince over us? Moreover, you have not brought us into a land flowing with milk and honey, nor given us inheritance of fields and vineyards?" [Numbers 16:13-14]

The whole situation was a mess! The next day, Korah, with the 250 Levites, and Aaron came to the Tabernacle. They took their censers with the incense and put fire in them to burn before the Lord. Immediately, the glory of the Lord appeared over the tabernacle.

God spoke to Moses and Aaron telling them to get away from Korah and the 250 Levites, because He was going to consume them. Moses and Aaron begged the Lord not to kill them, but the Lord insisted they get away. Then, the Lord told Moses and Aaron to get away from the tents of Korah, Dathan, and Abiram and to tell the rest of the Israelite community to get away.

Moses gives God's instructions to the Israelites:

"Hereby you shall know that the Lord has sent me to do all these works and that it has not been of my own accord. If these men die as all men die, or if they are visited by the fate of all mankind, then the Lord has not sent me. But if the Lord creates something new, and the ground opens its mouth and swallows them up with all that belongs to them, and they go down alive into Sheol, then you shall know that these men have despised the Lord." [Numbers 16:28-30]

As soon as Moses stopped speaking, the ground split apart under them, so that the families of Korah, Dathan, Abiram, and On and all their belongings were swallowed up by the earth. And then fire came out from the Lord and consumed the 250 Levites offering incense at the Tabernacle.

Let's pause this story for a moment and allow what just happened to settle in our minds. Yes. That just happened. I told you this was one of those biblical stories that we may not like. God just caused a giant sinkhole to open and swallow the families and possessions of the rebels and God just sent fireballs to kill the rebels at the Tabernacle.

But, remember God's framework of love. God chases us with radical, unrelenting love in the wilderness and in the Promised Land. It's framed by God's love and filled with God's love, even though we may not see love on the surface.

Right after the sinkhole and fireballs, the Lord instructs Moses to tell Eleazar, Aaron's son, to take the rebels censers out of the fire, because they had become holy. (More on this later, but essentially the censers carried incense that could only be used for the Lord and not for common uses.[30]) Eleazar was instructed to make the censers into "hammered plates as a covering for the altar, for they offered them before the Lord and they became holy."[31] These hammered plates would be placed over the altar as a sign for the people that only descendants of Aaron could burn incense before the Lord (a role that was only for the chosen high priest). If anyone who was not a descendant of Aaron burned incense before the Lord they would become like Korah and the 250 Levites.

I wish the story ended here. But, sometimes we don't always learn the first time.

The next day, the whole community of Israel complained against Moses and Aaron and blamed them for killing all the people. As Moses and Aaron stood in front of the tabernacle, a cloud fell and the glory of the Lord appeared. Again, then the Lord told Moses and Aaron to get away from the community, because He was going to kill them.

More fireballs coming out from the cloud of the Lord to kill the complaining Israelite community. (That'll teach us to be a little more mindful when we start complaining about what God is up to in our wilderness wanderings!)

Moses - forever the intercessor of this community - tells Aaron to take his censer, put fire on it from the altar, and lay incense in it to make atonement for the people, so that the fireballs would stop. Aaron ran into the midst of the people to offer up the incense. Standing between the living and the dead, Aaron made atonement for the Israelite community and the fireballs stopped. But not before 14,700 people who rose up in rebellion, like Korah and his followers, died.

Once the atonement was made and the fireballs stopped, God instructed Moses to bring a staff from the chiefs of all twelve tribes in the community. (Staffs were a symbol of leadership and authority in this ancient culture.) Each person was to write his name on the staff. Aaron was to write his name on the staff of the tribe of Levi. Once all of the staffs were gathered by Moses at the Tabernacle, the Lord would make the staff of the chosen high priest sprout. In this way, God would show them who was chosen, so they would stop complaining and rebelling.

The next day, Moses went into the Tabernacle where God made Aaron's staff sprout with buds, blossoms, and ripe almonds. Moses took all of the staffs and showed them to the people, so they could see Aaron's staff sprouted. The sprouted staff of Aaron revealed to the Israelite community that God chose Aaron as the high priest over the people.

The Lord told Moses:

> "Put back the staff of Aaron before the testimony, to be kept as a sign for the rebels, that you may make an end of their grumbling against me, lest they die." [Numbers 17:10]

Where am I?

As I have wrestled with this story and wrestled with my own wilderness wanderings, I uncover more questions than answers. Anytime I take time to explore my values, mindset, and vision, I emerge from that exploration with a sense of clarity about who I am. I uncover a deeper understanding of my God-design and my God-designed voice. And then, that deeper understanding is tested and refined in the wilderness of the tension. In the wilderness, the chasm between my God-design and my current reality feels extraordinarily deep and wide.

In one of my wilderness wanderings, I shared with a friend that I was feeling disoriented. From one week to the next, I went from feeling clarity to feeling loss and lost. She said: "It's interesting that you described yourself as being disoriented, because disorientation doesn't suggest confusion about who you are, but about where you are." Where was I?

Gaining clarity about our values, mindset, and vision focuses on "who am I?" Being in the tension shifts the focus to "where am I now and where am I going in light of my understanding of who I am?"

The hard work of uncovering our God-designed selves is only the first part of finding our voices. The second part is the hard work refining ourselves. In refinement, we align ourselves to our God-designed selves. Aligning ourselves to God is how we translate the revelations of our soul to the motivations of our feet. Alignment is about becoming fully integrated with ourselves. When where we are and where we're going doesn't seem to align with who we are and who we are becoming, that can feel disorienting. We can find ourselves, like the Israelites, in the wilderness wanderings of the tension.

In the story of the Israelites wilderness wanderings, three big questions emerge. Our exploration of these questions (where we may stumble upon more questions than answers) offer some insight into how to navigate the wilderness and allow it to refine our God-designed voices:

- Why are we prone to rebel against God in our wilderness wanderings?
- How does having a framework in our wilderness wanderings guide us?
- What are the kingdom principles of the framework in this story, and what do they reveal about how God is leading us through the wilderness wanderings?

Prone to Rebel

Why are we prone to rebel against God in our wilderness wanderings?

Perhaps the best way to begin to unravel this question is to reflect on what it means to rebel. At its most basic to rebel is to resist. Often the resistance is against an authority. This resistance against an authority usually happens because the authority has become oppressive and unjust. Our culture is filled with stories of resistance against injustice. From Harry Potter and Dumbledore's Army to Stars Wars and the Resistance to Black Lives Matter. We seem to glamorize and even encourage resistance. Truthfully, as an attorney passionate about civil rights, social justice, and advocacy, resistance is my playground. There are very real injustices in the world that ought to be met with resistance. Before we rush to rebellion, we ought to ask ourselves two questions: 1. What is the injustice that has been done and 2. What are the root feelings, beliefs, and/or thoughts in me that are stirring resistance? Another way to think of those questions is: What is at the root of my rebellion?

If we peel back the layers of the main people in the story of this rebellion, we may be able to make some inferences about the root of their resistance. When the story begins in the Bible, it begins with a genealogy. Now I know, genealogies in the Bible are really easy to skip. So and so, the son of so and so, the son of so and so. Blah, blah, blah. To us, it may read as an unimportant lists of names we can't pronounce and don't care about that get in the way of the real story.

But, in the Old Testament names and family trees tell stories by themselves. The people of Israel are one gigantic family that started with God's formation of Adam and Eve. As the family tree continues, we meet Jacob, who the Lord renamed Israel. Jacob had twelve sons who became the tribes of Israel. Just like our families have family drama, the tribes of Israel have a long history of drama that reaches into the story of Korah's rebellion in the wilderness.

> "Now Korah, the son of Izhar, son of Kohath, son of Levi, and Dathan and Abiram the sons of Eliab, and On the son of Peleth, sons of Reuben, took men." [Numbers 16:1]

Because of the significance of families among the tribes of Israel, this opening verse with its genealogy cannot be an accident. So, let's resist the temptation to read over it as a list of names we can't pronounce and don't care about it. Korah, Dathan, Abiram, and On are connected to specific families among the tribes of Israel. Their interesting family dynamics may help us understand the root of the resistance.

Korah was the son of Izhar who was the son of Kohath who was the son of Levi. If we trace Korah's lineage, we see he is a son of Levi. As we've talked about before, Levi, the fourth son of Jacob/Israel, was the tribe chosen to minister before the Lord in the Tabernacle. Digging into this family tree we find that, Kohath, Korah's grandfather, had four clans that belonged to him: the Amramites, the Izharites, the Herbonites, and the Uzzielites.[32] Korah was part of the second clan, the Izharites. The four clans of Kohath's family oversaw the south side of the Tabernacle by caring for the ark, the table, the lampstand, the altars, the vessels of the sanctuary the priests used to minister, and the screen. Elizaphan, an Uzzielite from the fourth clan, was placed as the chief over all of Kohath's clans.[33] In this Hebrew culture, the last and youngest would never be chosen as the chief of the tribe. Generally, this was a right of the firstborn and if something happened to disqualify the firstborn, it certainly would not have gone to the last born. It would have gone in order of succession. Meaning that Korah should've been in line for leadership long before Elizaphan. So, how is it that Elizaphan, an Uzzielite from the last and youngest clan, was placed as the chief?

Put yourself in Korah's shoes for a moment. You live in a culture where it's an expected custom of the order of succession for leadership among your family. You are passed over for leadership in favor of your little cousin from the youngest clan! This goes against everything that you know about how things are supposed to work. And if you're real honest with yourself, you may feel some strong feelings of resistance about this "injustice" done to you. Your expectations were broken and you were overlooked as someone to lead your family. It's like you didn't get the promotion that was "supposed" to be yours. Instead, someone who is both under-qualified and unqualified gets promoted. Maybe some of you are thinking: "Whatever, more responsibilities for him!" But, this was a cultural expectation and a birthright for Korah.

I don't know if your expectations have ever been broken and you've ever felt unseen, but every time that's ever happened to me, I took it personally. I was supposed to be the first chair of our orchestra in high school. My whole life set me up for that expectation. And then Jordan Fletcher moved to town and I was passed over for a seat that was supposed to be mine!! (Now that I got that mini rant out of my system, Jordan if you're reading this, no hard feelings!)

When our expectations are broken we may get defensive. Things were supposed to be a certain way and now they're not. We wonder if we were unseen because there's a deficit in us. A little voice inside us says: "You're not enough." We may feel rejected and unwanted. All of those feelings, if left unexamined, can cause us to become hardened inside and to project that pain externally onto others. We look for someone or something to blame. (Jordan Fletcher!) We convince ourselves that because the "rights" that were supposed to be ours have been taken away from us, an "injustice" has been done to us by "them". We deserved "x" and now we are hurt, frustrated, and resistant to whoever caused this "injustice."

Here's a truth I'm learning all the time: Just because I have an expectation of something, doesn't mean that I have a right to that thing. My frustration about an injustice done to me is often based on a falsely constructed reality. My perceptions and misconceptions do not justify my resistance against others and my rebellion against God.

Before we go any further, I want to acknowledge that you may not be someone who takes broken expectations and being unseen personally. I don't want to project that feeling on to you. But in the case of this story and the Hebraic cultural expectations, we could draw an inference that Korah took personally the "injustice" of Moses and Aaron "putting themselves in charge." This was yet another time where his expectations were broken and he was passed over for a place of leadership. Korah takes the "injustice" that's been done to him and does three destructive things:

1. He rallied three powerful and important allies: Dathan, Abiram, and On (three Reubenites who had their own family drama related to unmet expectations and being overlooked).[34]
2. He convinced 250 well-known Levites that an "injustice" had been done to them.
3. He gathered all of these people to speak against Moses and Aaron.

God is justice. God cannot be unjust towards us. It's not in His nature. When we're wandering in the wilderness going through situations we do no understand where we may feel, like Korah, that God has been unjust towards us we need to get curious about the root of our resistance. Those feelings, if left unexamined, can cause hardness to overcome our hearts. A heart hardness that can cause us to speak against each other through a falsely constructed reality. We think we're resisting an "injustice", but really we're rebelling against God. A rebellion against God is a rebellion against our God-designed selves. This kind of rebellion can distort our God-designed voices to the point of becoming destructive. Korah shows us how our God-designed voice can become destructive in our wilderness wanderings when we don't examine the root of our resistance.

Let the Framework Be Your Guide

How does having a framework in our wilderness wanderings guide us?

Understanding God's frameworks help us to see God's ways even when we can't see the way. God's framework of love begins and ends this story. But somehow Korah and those who joined in the rebellion lost sight of that love. When they lost sight of God's framework of love, the wilderness wanderings made no sense to them and the path to the promise seemed unclear. They allowed where they were to distort their understanding of who they were.

When Korah and the Levites spoke against Moses and Aaron, Moses reponds with an insightful reminder of who they were:

> "Is it too small a thing for you that the God of
> Israel has separated you from the congregation of

> Israel, to bring you near to himself, to do service
> in the tabernacle of the Lord and to stand before
> the congregation to minister to them, and that he
> has brought you near him, and all your brothers
> the sons of Levi with you?" [Numbers 16:9-10]

Moses reminds them: you've already been separated, you already belong, and you already have a significant role. He reminds them that God brought them near already out of His framework of love. Korah and the 250 Levites, lost sight of themselves as God saw them. They assumed that God had lost sight of them, because who they were didn't align with where they found themselves. They were wandering in circles in the wilderness following the leadership of Moses and Aaron. Their perceptions of where they were distorted their perspective of who they were.

They went down the destructive path of determining who they were based on where they were. They also determined who they were by measuring themselves against Aaron and Moses. Moses asks the Levites: "What is Aaron that you grumble against him?"[35] Notice that Moses doesn't say "who" is Aaron. I don't think that's a grammatical accident on Moses's part. We cannot measure who we are based on who someone else is. Their God-design is their God-design and our God-design is our God-design. When Moses asks "what is Aaron that you grumble against him" he's asking: what significance does Aaron have over who you are? The interrogatory word used here, "what", implies that the object of the question is insignificant. Their perceptions of Aaron distorted their perspective of themselves.

When Moses tried to speak to Dathan and Abiram, they refused and sent a messenger saying:

"Is it a small thing that you have brought us up out of a land flowing with milk and honey, to kill us in the wilderness; that you must also make yourself a prince over us? Moreover, you have not brought us into a land flowing with milk and honey, nor given us inheritance of fields and vineyards. Will you put out the eyes of these men? We will not come up." [Numbers 16:13-14]

Dathan and Abiram measured themselves against who Moses was. They allege that Moses brought them into the wilderness to kill them, that he hadn't brought them into a land flowing with milk and honey, and that he hadn't given them an inheritance. In addition, to all of these statements being false perceptions, they also fail to recognize that it wasn't Moses who brought them into the wandering wilderness. The text tells us that Moses gets "very angry" after hearing this message. He tells the Lord: "I have not taken one donkey from them, and I have not harmed one of them."[36] Essentially Moses is saying: Don't blame me for your false perception of where you are and where you're going.

God's frameworks keep us from allowing where we are to distort our understanding of who we are. Who we are is not determined by where we are. The standard for who we are is not other people. Moses spoke the truth of God's framework of love in the midst of the wilderness wanderings, but they couldn't hear his voice. In the wilderness, we have choices about which voices we listen to and guide us. The voices we listen to either lead us to God's voice or away from God's voice. What voices are you listening to? Are you listening to voices that point to God's framework of love?

When who you are doesn't align with where you are, listen to the right voices. Listen to the voices that lead you back to God's framework of love. God's framework of love in your wilderness wanderings is meant to lead you. As you find yourself wandering in the wilderness God may seem distant or absent. But His love is still framing your experiences, so that your experiences don't distort who you are. The framework of God's love keeps you from determining who you are based on where you are. Where you are is temporary and who you are is eternal. The framework of God's love stops you from measuring yourself against other people. When you don't know the way, the framework of God's love leads you towards His way.

Kingdom Principles

What are the Kingdom principles of God's framework in the story of Korah and the rebellion?
What do the Kingdom principles reveal about how God is leading us through the wilderness wanderings?

God's frameworks always contain Kingdom principals. Kingdom principles are threads that hold God's framework together. They provide us with points of reference to understand how God is working within His frameworks. Because the Word of God is both a book of promises and principles, we must look for these points of reference. They are markers that operate within God's framework to lead us on the path to His promises. Three Kingdom principles in particular are threaded throughout this story. They are markers that lead us within God's love towards God's promise.

Kingdom Principle: God's ways are not our ways

Korah and the people who rebelled seemed to be skeptical that God's hand could possibly be leading them through these wilderness wanderings. They seem to have a different perspective about how God operates than how God actually operates. In their minds, "all in the congregation are holy"[37], so what made Moses and Aaron think they could assume the position of leadership. They seemed to feel they, as Levites, had as much "right" to lead the people and minister before the Lord as Moses and Aaron. Nothing about this situation conformed to their ways. In their minds, they should've already arrived in the Promised Land.

The more that I dig into this story, the more I get the sense that the folks who rebelled were trying to get control over a situation that didn't make sense to them. They were trying to make sense of a wilderness that did not look like God's promises. The wilderness looked more like a path to nowhere, then a path to the promise. Where's the land flowing with milk and honey? It's not this. So, what do we have to do to get there?

I can relate to the rebels. When I can't make sense of the ways things are happening, I attempt to grasp at the things to control the situation. What do I have to do to get to where I'm supposed to be? I can go into troubleshoot and fix-it mode. Trying to control my way through the wilderness seems easier than surrendering to God's ways through the wilderness. But even in the midst of the wilderness, I have choices. I can choose to live in the midst of the promise. I can choose to remember that God's ways are not my ways. These choices make all the difference in how I navigate my wilderness wanderings.

The people who rebelled tried to control their way through the wilderness by trying to overtake Moses and Aaron. In their attempt to control their way through the wilderness, they continued to persist in resistance to God's ways.

Sometimes the greatest way we wander through the wilderness is to persist in surrender. That may sound counterintuitive. But persisting in surrender to God's ways frees us to wander intentionally. We can't reduce God's ways to our finite understanding. When we try to control ways that we do not fully understand, we're trying to make sense of the infinite. God's infinite perspective is clear only to God. Any attempt to take control of what is only clear to God results in us aimlessly wandering, because we have no idea where we're going. Persistent surrender to the Kingdom principle that God's ways are not my ways, frees us to depend on God and allows us to intentionally wander. We may not know the way, but we know God's ways are always leading us to Him.

Moses understood this level of persistent surrender. "Hereby you shall know that the Lord has sent me to do all these works, and that it has not been of my own accord."[38]

God's ways are not our ways. Moses attests to this Kingdom principle. He didn't try to control their way through the wilderness. Instead, He points to the Lord. God sent me. These are God's ways, not my ways. There's a freedom in this kind of persistent surrender. There's a freedom to be led by God. Yes, Moses was the chosen leader, but what made him a powerful leader was that he was a follower of God's ways. Moses may not have understood where he was, but because he understand who he was he didn't have to question God's ways. There is a freedom in persistent surrender to God's ways.

Kingdom Principle: God listens and responds

There's a detail in the way that Moses surrenders to God's ways that reveals another Kingdom principle threaded into God's framework. Moses tells the people that they will know that the Lord sent him if God creates something new and the ground opens its mouth and swallows them. Moses had no way of knowing that

God would do exactly what he said, but God did. Remember, the giant sinkhole. Moses spoke it and God did it.

God listens and responds when we speak things into existence. The stories we read throughout the Bible reveal this Kingdom principle. We see people in a relationship with God speaking things into existence and God listening and responding to what they've spoken. The God-designed voice of a righteous person is powerful and effective. God listens and responds.

We see God listen and respond to Aaron also. After the Lord creates a sinkhole to swallow the people, they kept rebelling. So, God sends another round of fireballs to kill the rebels. Moses tells Aaron to intercede for the Israelites. Aaron takes the censer and runs into the midst of the people to intercede for them. As Aaron stood in the midst of the people interceding for them, the fireballs stopped.

This must have been a chaotic moment! People running everywhere while fireballs came out of a cloud. Yet, Aaron runs into the chaos to intercede for the people before the Lord. And what happens? The Lord listens and responds to his intercession, so that more people don't die as a consequence for their rebellion.

God listens and responds when we speak in alignment with who we are even in the midst of the chaos of where we are. The intercession was in alignment with who Aaron was and the God-designed voice that Aaron uncovered inside himself. How amazing that the God of the universe stops sending fireballs towards rebellious people, because He listens and responds to someone speaking according to his God-design and Kingdom principles.

Even in the midst of my own wilderness wanderings, if I'm speaking according to my God-designed voice, God listens and responds to me. God listens and responds to make manifest the things that I need to navigate the wilderness. Yes, even in the wilderness, God listens and responds.

Kingdom Principle: God provides signs

After God consumes the people who joined the rebellion, He provides a sign to show that He was with them in their wilderness wanderings. He instructs Moses to tell Eleazar, Aaron's son, to take the censers the rebels used out of the fire, because the censers became holy. The censers were to be hammered into plates that would be placed over the altar as a frame to cover the altar. This sign would remind people that no outsider, who is not of the descendants of Aaron, should burn incense before the Lord. Perhaps at first glance this seems meaningless or even strange. Why would the Lord instruct that these censers be taken from the fire and converted into hammered plates to cover the altar? How had they become holy?

Let's rewind a little bit here. Remember when we talked about how burning incense to the Lord was the highest function of the priesthood? Back in Exodus 30 when the Lord and Moses talk about the Tabernacle, God says that once the Tabernacle is anointed with oil, the utensils used "will become holy."[39] God goes on to say that the utensils were holy and the incense could not be used for individual or common purposes, because it "shall be most holy."[40] When the 250 rebels used the censers, they become set apart for the Lord. But, instead of continuing to use them as censers, God instructs that they are recreated into a bronze hammered plate. Hammered into a plate that would be used as covering for the altar and a sign to remind the people of who could come near to the Lord to serve as the high priest and intercessor.

The second sign God gives happens after the people rebel (again) and 14,700 of them are consumed by fireballs. The Lord instructs Moses to tell each tribe to bring a staff and that the Lord would cause the staff of the one He chose to sprout. The following day, Aaron's staff from the house of Levi, sprouted and put forth buds and blossoms and bore ripe almonds. In this way, the Lord created a sign that Aaron was in fact chosen as the high priest and they ought to stop complaining. A staff - a broken branch of a tree - sprouted with flowers and almonds! God sprouted life out of barrenness. Through this miracle, the Lord provides a sign that He was present in the wilderness wanderings. Aaron's sprouted staff was placed in the Ark of the Covenant inside the holy of holies in the tabernacle.

While the sprouted staff was a symbol of God's choosing Aaron, the Lord seemed to be revealing a greater sign in that staff. God's sign of the sprouted staff became a symbol that God will fulfill His purposes His ways. This staff - a broken branch of a tree - had no hope of sprouting, because it was not connected to a root system. But, the Lord made it sprout. And not only did it sprout blossoms, but it sprouted almonds. Almonds are one of the first fruits of the springtime season after the winter and a symbol of hope. God's signs in the wilderness mark the way of hope. Hope that the wilderness is only temporary. The wilderness is a season that will pass.

Only God could create life as a sign of His presence in the desert. Only God can offer the kind of hope that when you don't see the way you can still see His ways. Only God could bring you through the wilderness wandering of the tension. God provides signs. As we wander through the wilderness, God uses signs to help us see His ways even when we can't see the way.

We can't edit the wilderness out of our stories. It's often in the parts of our story that don't make any sense, where God refines our voices. When we feel disoriented about where we are, it's tempting to rebel. It's tempting to look for someone or something to blame or attack. But who we are is not defined by where we are. In our wilderness wanders, our God-designed voices must be led by God's frameworks. God's framework of love ought to serve as the beginning and the end of our wilderness wanderings. As we are led by God's framework, we must speak according to His Kingdom principles. Because as we speak according to His principles, even though we may not see the way, we wander intentionally according to God's way towards His promises.

Color You _____ Moment

Questions to Ponder:

- What is an area of your life that you are prone to rebel against God?
- How would God speak who you are into the area of your life where you are prone to rebel against God?
- How can you speak what God says about who you are into your own life?
- How can the Kingdom Principles in this story lead you forward and encourage you in the tension?

TWISTED TRUTHS. DISTORTED DIRECTIONS. BLURRED LINES.

"I am loyal to the throne. What are you loyal to?" // *Okoye to Nakia,*
Black Panther

People claim there's no such thing as an undercover Christian. Except, I was one. I've read and studied Jesus's words inviting his followers to not hide their light or lose their saltiness. I've preached and taught these truths, even in the midst of seasons when living this fully integrated life feels impossible. The tension between God's promises and their fulfillment can seem like an endless season. In the seemingly endless wandering, we can become lured into undercover Christianity wondering: "what am I doing here, God?" We can lose our grip on the hope that once fueled our faith and the grace that once sustained our relationship with God. The loss of tenacity in the tension can jeopardize our God-design and God-designed voice. And that's what happened to me.

"Since When Do You Go to Church?"
During my final year of law school, I worked for a legal civil rights nonprofit working on a project with small business owners. The small team at the nonprofit was a close knit community. If you've

ever worked in a small office, you may have experienced that sense that from day one everyone is very familial. Every Monday, my supervisor and other colleagues asked about my weekend. For a majority of the 3-month internship, I told them about my weekend, but I always left out the part about spending all of my Sundays in church and serving as the leader of our middle school ministry. Essentially, I left out half of my weekend. At the time, I wasn't 100% sure why I left out a huge part of my life. I justified it by thinking that my colleagues would see me differently and judge me. Even though my colleagues and my supervisor, in particular, always left a door open to share differing opinions and respected differences. Not sharing about a huge part of my life felt uncomfortable and inauthentic, but I still never shared.

I am naturally an under-sharer. I generally do not share a lot about myself with other people. But this wasn't under-sharing. This was an intentional decision to be undercover.

Then one Monday, it slipped. We were talking about racial profiling. I started sharing a story one of my young people shared at church. This young person felt their teacher disciplined them unfairly because they were one of the few Latinx students in the class. Before I could even finish the story, my supervisor stopped me, with a confused look on her face, and asked me: "Wait, since when do you go to church? And since when do you work with youth?"

Our conversation took a very different turn. I'd worked at this organization for about 2 months already and no one knew that I was a Christian, much less than I led the middle school ministry in my church. My supervisor asked me all kinds of questions about my faith and shared about her background with the Church. She was fascinated, wondering how I could be "so liberal and still believe in God", wondering why I hadn't shared about my

98

faith prior to now, wondering how on earth I worked with young people, and on and on. This was such a huge part of my life and I hadn't shared it, not because I was under-sharing, but because I felt I had to keep it undercover.

When we receive the grace of salvation, we begin a relationship with God where God invites us to live according to a new standard. The unmerited favor of God - that rescues us from trying to live life out of our own broken strength - awakens us to live by a standard that aligns with our God-design. God's standard has always been and will always be holiness. Holiness is being set apart as sacred to the Lord as we become more like the Lord. We are instructed: "Be holy, for I am holy."[41] The invitation to holiness is an invitation to follow the Lord's model of being and doing. Living in holiness is not meant to be burdensome. Jesus tells us living by the holiness standard is a yoke that is easy and light.[42] Speaking to an agrarian community, through this invitation the people understood the yoke as a heavy wooden frame laid on top of animals limiting their movement in a particular direction as they pulled a heavy load or plowed through dirt. Because two animals were joined together, they could better pull the heavy load or more easily plow through the dirt. In the same way, when we are joined together with Christ, we are better able to live according to the holiness standard and as a result, live according to our God-design. Taking on Christ's yoke, we don't have to exert so much energy living out of our own strength. We live with and out of our relationship with Christ. We learn from Christ's example and as we learn from Christ we become more like Christ. The yoke becomes easy and light, because it's a perfect fit for our authentic God-design and it's guiding us to our God-designed voice. Living in His holiness leads to us speaking with our truest voice.

In the tension, the struggle comes when the grace that once compelled us to live according to the holiness standard feels insufficient. We come into seasons where our recollection of God's grace feels vague and distant. Our present tension pulls us into our former ignorance of God's holiness standard. We see this happen to the Israelites as they go through the tension between God's promises and their fulfillment.

After Korah's rebellion, where God reveals some Kingdom principles of His framework, the Israelites wandered through the desert for 38 years before we get another glimpse into their story. In Numbers 25, we meet the Israelites after 38 years of obscurity, living in Shittim. Shittim was a valley in the land of the Moabites where the Israelites set up camp before they crossed the Jordan River into the Promised Land. (I often wonder if on the border of the fulfillment of God's promises is where He reminds us of the holiness standard most emphatically. I wonder if He does this, because we cannot truly possess the promises, unless we've fully surrendered to God's standard for our lives. I wonder if it's in these challenges places, that God calls us back to holiness, so that on the other side of the challenges our voices are aligned with our calling.) Here in Shittim - the last place the Israelites would live before entering the Promised Land - the Lord reminds them what it looks like to be set apart as sacred to the Lord as we become more like the Lord.

Don't Get It Twisted

In Shittim, the Israelites camped on the border of the Promised Land. It was also on the border of the land occupied by the Moabites. Leading up to the story in Numbers 25, the king of the Moabites, Balak, fearing the threat of an Israelite takeover, commissions a seer, Balaam, to curse the Israelites. However, in this series of events, including a talking donkey, the Lord mysteriously interrupts every curse towards the Israelites with a blessing for the Israelites. Then, Numbers 25 opens with a vivid image of the ways the Moabites manipulated the Israelites to curse themselves by distorting God's standards of holiness.

> "While Israel lived in Shittim the people began to whore with the daughters of Moab."[43]

When God rescued the Israelites from slavery, He invited them into an intimate relationship of communion where they would be set apart as sacred to the Lord. And yet they cheated on the Lord. The Moabite women invited the Israelite men to compromise themselves sexually and spiritually. They invited the Israelites to commit adultery and to attend sacrificial feasts for their pagan gods. Instead of remaining yoked, or joined, to the Lord, Israel yoked themselves to Baal of Peor, a pagan sex god. By accepting this invitation, the Israelites rejected their relationship with God and God's invitation to live in intimacy. As a result, the anger of the Lord burned against the Israelites. The Lord instructed Moses to hang all of the leaders "in the sun."[44] Moses gave an additional instruction to the judges to kill each of the men that joined themselves to Baal of Peor.

Maybe when you hear the opening part of this story you ask yourself: "Why is God being so harsh on the Israelites? So what, they had sex with non-Israelites?" Just as with the story of Korah's rebellion, our gut reaction to this story may be to become resistant to God's word and become tempted to want to edit this out of the Bible. We may wonder where our understanding of the mercy, grace, love, and kindness of God can be found in texts that don't make sense to our cultural lens of right and wrong, good and evil, and justice and peace.

In the tension between God's promises and their fulfillment, we can become susceptible to temptations that distort the clear instructions God has given us. When we don't understand the place God has brought us to - because it looks nothing like the promises He made to us - we can tend to distort the word God gave us. A disorienting place can lead us to distort our purpose. A distorted purpose twists our God-design selves and our God-designed voice. We say "yes" to the things that we once said "no" to and we add our voice to conversations that we once would never have been part of. Instead of our voice speaking in truth, we speak in distortions.

This is where the Israelites find themselves on the border of the Promised Land. The instructions God gave them were designed to lead them into the freedom of the Promised Land, but they compromised those instructions. In Leviticus 18, God gave the Israelites instructions about sex and sexuality that were very different from how the culture of the time understood sex and sexuality. In this historical moment, sexual immorality was profoundly distorted. This distortion of sexuality led to moral confusion and spiritual chaos. Our bodies are just as spiritual as our souls. The body and soul are intimately connected and we are deeply spiritual beings. In God's great compassion and understanding of how he designed humanity, He gave the Israelites moral laws to lead the Israelites to an understanding of how to relate to God and one another. Ultimately, these instructions were about how to live in freedom and abundance. They were about supporting the Israelites to live in intimacy with their Creator.

In the disorienting places that we can find ourselves in the tension, instead of being tenacious, we can become tempted to twist God's instructions. Even when we don't understand why we are in a disorienting place that does not give us the green light to distort the instructions God gave us as we walk towards his promises.

Tenacity in the tension is as much about holding on to the promise as it is about embracing the truth that we are transforming into people who can possess the promise. This transformation happens as we learn to conform to God's holiness standard and not twist the standard for our own comfort. Our God-designed selves look like Him and conform to Him. They do not look like us forcing God to conform to our image and comforts.

When the places that we find ourselves in cause us to become disoriented about our purpose, we may think that God's instructions have become ambiguous. We can imagine that after 38 years of wandering in the wilderness, in utter obscurity, the Israelites may have felt they were in a season of ambiguity, wondering "why God?" Maybe they lost hope in the promise. Maybe they lost sight of the grace that once compelled them.

We know they were on the border of possessing the Promised Land, because we have the advantage of seeing what happens next in the story. This was not their perspective. They had been in the tension for so long that perhaps they could not see that the promise was in sight. If you have you ever felt hopeless or you've lost appreciation for grace, then you can relate to the Israelites. You can understand the deep disorientation that led them to get it twisted.

Twisted truths. Distorted directions. Blurred lines. This is where the Israelites found themselves as they allowed themselves to be seduced by the Moabites, instead of secured by God. They yoked themselves to Baal of Peor.[45] In this ancient culture, the term "yoked" was a term used to describe a woman with two lovers. In this duplicitous devotion, the people of Israel became yoked as servants to their new master, Baal of Peor. They allowed their God-design identity and voice to become disoriented by the direction of a created god, instead of the uncreated God who invited them into a relationship with him. The text doesn't tell us how the Midianite women seduced the Israelites, but something about their invitation was so compelling that they joined themselves to a god who wasn't their god. When they did this, they set themselves on a path that polluted how God was preparing them to possess the promise. Instead of moving in the direction of God, they moved in the direction of an illusion of god. The Lord was angered.

Distortion leads to pain. Pain, because something is being twisted into a false form. Pain, because something is being transformed against its design. When the Creator saw His creation becoming distorted, He burned with anger. Who could blame Him? The pain of seeing the ones He invited into an intimate relationship, turned their back on Him. They twisted their design and as a result, twisted His perfect purposes for them.

So, God instructs the chief leaders to be hung in the sun. What a poignant detail and instruction. The chiefs of the people - the leaders of the community - would be held out as an example and hung in the light for all to see the impact of their distorted behavior. What happened in the darkness would now become exposed in the light. God sees all. This isn't meant to creep us out. It's meant to reveal to us that God cares so much about every area of our lives that He's watching mindfully and lovingly. God doesn't want to have a little impact on one area of our lives. The invitation to live according to holiness is an invitation for every area of our life, so that our whole lives can be wholly and fully integrated. God invites us to total transformation, so that we can find full integration with our authentic selves.

On the border of the Lord's promise for them, the Israelites accepted a seductive invitation. What invitations do we accept that distort the holiness we've been called towards? The invitations may come in the form of relationships, of experiences, or even mindsets. Each of these different kinds of invitations may not seem threatening, but anything that compromises our relationship with our Creator compromises our holiness. When the promises of God seem as though they may never become our realities, invitations that appeal to our immediate wants, doubts, weaknesses, and longings may be the most seductive and distorting.

I started working at the legal civil rights nonprofit during my last year of law school. I went to law school thinking that I was going to be a labor lawyer, then thinking I was going to be an immigration lawyer, and then thinking what am I going to do? At this point, I knew that I had an interest in working with small businesses. But up until that point, because I thought I was going to do something in civil rights, I hadn't taken classes that prepared me to work with small businesses. Not to mention, that I wasn't even clear on what it would mean to work with small business on legal business matters. And now, I had 9 months to figure it all out.

Working with small businesses at this nonprofit felt like the silver bullet towards figuring it all out. A few weeks into the role working, sitting in a frigid backroom in a corner that felt like a cave, I thought, "what am I doing here?" I'm no clearer now on what I want to do after I graduated law school. All the while, I was leading the middle school ministry in my church and feeling pulled to ministry in ways I had never felt. I felt hopeless about the future, ambiguous about what was next, and frustrated with God. How could God bring me basically to the end of law school without giving me any clarity on what was coming next?

I started to doubt. I doubted whether I should've gone to law school in the first place - did I read God wrong? I doubted whether I was going to find any jobs after law school - did God forget me? I doubted whether I should've moved to Boston at all - did God want me here? These questions replayed on a loop in my mind. They took me to a place of distorting God's word, instead of depending on God's truth. Instead of seeing the opportunity of this role and how I may be on the edge of what's next, I was frustrated. Frustration kept me undercover. Twisted truths. Distorted directions. Blurred lines.

Redefining Jealousy

As the Lord's anger burned against the Israelites for their compromising behaviors, Zimri, the son of a chief of the Simeonites tribe, brought Cozbi, the daughter of a tribal leader of the Midianites, into his home. Zimri brought Cozbi into his home in front of Moses and all of the people of Israel despite the plague that was bringing destruction to the Israelites. Then Phinehas, Aaron's grandson, saw it, rose up, left the congregation, took a spear, went into the bedroom where they were and drove the spear through both Zimri and Cozbi. Immediately the plague ceased, but not before killing 24,000 people. Because of Phinehas's jealousy for the Lord's jealousy[46], the Lord said:

> "Behold, I give to him my covenant of peace and
> it shall be to him and to his descendants after him
> the covenant of a perpetual priesthood, because
> he was jealous for his God and made atonement
> for the people of Israel." [Numbers 25:12-13]

There is a stark contrast between the defiant unholiness of Zimri and Cozbi and the jealous holiness of Phinehas. There was a plague raging throughout the Israelites camp as a result of their distortion of God's directions and Zimri, in utter defiance to God, brings a Midianite woman into the bedroom of his tent where his family was and in the sight of all of the people. The entire camp knew the gravity did not compel holiness. For Zimri, it compelled further defiance.

If we read this scene carefully, the major characters are described in relations to their family tree. (Remember, earlier we talked about the importance of family trees in Israelite culture.) In this family tree description, we are reminded that it was not the generation brought out of Egypt that would possess the Promised Land, but their children and their children's children. The text doesn't tell us this, but I wonder if the reason this small descriptive detail is given to us about the two major characters' family trees helps us discover a potential reason for Zimri's defiance and Phinehas's holiness.

The text tells us that Zimri was the son of Salu, a chief of a father's house belonging to the Simeonites.[47] Phinehas was the son of Eleazar who was the son of Aaron belonging to the Levites.[48] Simeon and Levi, two sons of Jacob and Leah, were blood brothers, unlike the many half-brothers that made up the tribes of Israel. And yet, despite this closeness in their family tree, we see them making different decisions in their storylines that lead them to play different roles among the people of Israel.

The Bible doesn't give us any details about Zimri's upbringing, but if we trace trends in the story of humanity, there are certain things that may lead someone to lack reverence for God. A lack of revelation, relationship, and responsibility can lead to someone having a lack of reverence. In Hebrew culture, they practiced the oral tradition where the stories, promises, and covenant of God were passed down from one generation to the next.

Had Zimri heard the stories and received the revelation of God and God's promises to His father's generation? Had Zimri accepted the invitation to be in relationship with this incredible God? Had he understood the implications and responsibilities of that invitation? Did his lack of revelation, relationship, and responsibility cause him to have a lack of reverence for the holiness that God sought to instill in His people when the plague raged through the camp? My guess is that much like the trends we can trace throughout humanity, when we have a lack of revelation of, relationship with, and responsibility to God, it's challenging to revere God.

In contrast, Phinehas, the son of Eleazar, the son of Aaron, belonging to the Levites, seemed to have a revelation of God and the promise's God made to his father's and grandfather's generation. Perhaps, Phinehas's revelation came as a result of watching his family serving daily in the tabernacle, overseeing the holy instruments used in worship to God, and purifying themselves to practice their priestly duties. Phinehas probably responded to this revelation by accepting the invitation to enter into relationship with this holy God. He likely understood the responsibilities that came with that relationship, which is why we see him respond to those responsibilities with reverence during the plague that overcame the Israelites. His priestly role made him a public figure and gave him public authority among the Israelites. Let me be clear: the holiness standard in this text is not advocating for us to pick up spears and kill people. But there is a revelation in Phinehas's actions that cannot be overlooked: Holiness is an act of reverence.

When we revere someone, we respect them. We aren't afraid of them. We stand in awe of them. Reverence values relationship. In this story, reverence of God was a priority for Phinehas. We learn that reverence of God never jeopardize communion with God. This reverence knows that no matter where we go, what we do, or how we do it, God's presence is present. Do you revere God? Phinehas shows us that reverence of God leads to Godly jealously.

Godly jealousy is what pursued the Israelites in the first place and it's what pursues us. God had such a deep preference for us that His steadfast love prioritized us over all creation to be His. Godly jealousy protects, guards, and covers us. In the tension, Phinehas gives us an example of what it looks like to protect, guard, and cover the promises of God in the midst of disorientation and the temptation of distortion. God says: "Let your steadfast love prioritize Me over all creation. Protect, guard, and cover yourselves to ensure that My promises are fulfilled in your lives. Be set apart as sacred for Me." Holiness is rooted in Godly jealous. Holiness is not about our agenda, our preferences, or our ambitions. When we are jealous with God's jealousy we prioritize His ways, His glory, His purposes for His sake.

This Godly jealousy, led God to make a covenant of peace with Phinehas and his descendants. The covenant was one of perpetual priesthood. The covenant gave Phinehas and his descendants the authority to meditate and bring reconciliation between God and His people. The covenant made Phinehas and his descendants peacemakers and peacekeepers. The family of Levites received the promise of perpetual priesthood. But now, the general promise becomes connected to Phinehas and his descendants. Phinehas and his descendants become set apart as sacred to the Lord for the purposes of bringing peace. (An important side note about this covenant: The direct lineage of Phinehas merges with the Jesus Christ, the Prince of Peace later on in the story.) What a beautiful end to this story. A covenant of peace sealed in the tension, as a result of someone who sought to live according to the holiness standard. Phinehas teaches us that being set apart as sacred for the Lord as we become more like the Lord is Godly jealousy born out of reverence for God. When we live in holiness, like Phinehas, we can become the peacemakers and the peacekeepers for people.

Commitment Flows Out of Surrender

If we fast forward to Moses's final words to the Israelites before they enter the Promised Land, he brings up this scene at Shittim as a crucial moment for the Israelites to remember. In Deuteronomy 4, he recalls the way the Israelites "whored themselves to Baal of Peor" saying:

> "Your eyes have seen what the Lord did at Baal-peor, for the Lord your God destroyed from among you all the men who followed the Baal of Peor. But you who held fast to the Lord your God are all alive today. See, I have taught you statutes and rules, as the Lord my God commanded me that you should do them in the land that you are entering to take possession of it. Keep them and do them, for that will be your wisdom and your understanding in the sight of the peoples, who, when they hear all these statutes will say, "Surely this great nation is a wise and understanding people." [Deuteronomy 4:3-6]

Moses encourages those who lived after the plague at Baal-peor to hold fast to holiness. They lived and would enter the promise, because they were yoked to the Lord. This generation was set apart as sacred to the Lord and experienced the fullness living in their God-design, because they did not compromise the holiness standard. Holiness asks us to separate ourselves from distortions, to be jealous with Godly jealousy, and to remain committed to His commandments. When the Lord invites us to live by the holiness standard, He's inviting us to commit to living according to His ways.

I think one of the reasons we struggle so much with holiness is because we fear commitment. Commitment flows out of surrender. Surrender of ourselves, our ways, our desires, and our everything. Committing to any kind of relationship requires surrender. But here's the thing about surrender: Surrender doesn't come from a place of insecurity. Surrender is not about losing our identity or our voice in someone or something else. To fully surrender, we must be fully secure about ourselves, our identity, and our voice. If we aren't secure in who we are, then we aren't surrendering, we're sidestepping. Sidestepping happens when we become avoidant of someone or something. When we sidestep in relationships, we move ourselves out of the way from a place of insecurity or fear. Sidestepping leads to the other person in the relationship taking up all the space and us losing ourselves.

When we talk about surrendering to God, sometimes we make the mistake of talking about it in terms of diminishing ourselves. We think that surrender means allowing God to take up all the space and lose ourselves completely. That's not surrender. That's sidestepping. God is not interested in erasing who we are. God wants to exalt the fullness of who He created us to be. And that only comes through true surrender. True surrender happens when we yield our whole selves boldly and safely into the hands of God. When we surrender, we aren't diminishing ourselves, we're bringing the fullness of what we know about ourselves to the Lord, so that together we can become the fullness of our God-design. Surrender flows from security.

Bold surrender is an act of holiness where we can commit to His commandments. In our commitment to holiness, we find a freedom to securely hold fast to the steadfast ways that bring us into His promises.

Moses makes a connection between joining themselves to the commandments and their wisdom and understanding in the sight of the people. I hear many people call followers of Christ foolish for obeying a God that we can't see. I've had conversations with people who claim to follow Christ and water down the high call of holiness. But, the promise that I read here reveals that wisdom and understanding will be credited to those who commit to a life of holiness. The wisdom and understanding will be acknowledged not from other Israelites, but comes from the people of surrounding, unbelieving nations. This ought to encourage us in the tension, because the voices of those who commit to holiness will be the wisdom and understanding for a culture seeking everywhere for wisdom and understanding. When we go through the tension, living according to the holiness standard, refines our voices to speak with wisdom and understanding that the people in our lives need to hear.

Just before I graduated from law school, my former supervisor from the legal nonprofit called me. She asked if I wanted to do a post-graduate fellowship. She was going away on maternity leave and wanted me to help lead the small business project. I accepted the position.

I often wonder if the reason that she called me out of the blue to offer me that position had something to do with the fact that I stopped being undercover. It may not have been, but I know that the day I stopped being undercover was a turning point for me and for our relationship. I chose to not live led by doubt, but to see through my doubt with my faith. I made a decision to not twist God's truths. I committed to not distorting God's clear directions to me. I resolved to not compromise my calling to holiness by blurring the lines of my calling.

When I started working at that nonprofit, my faith and involvement in church became a natural conversation piece at the office. Every day, I was asked about my faith and about my work with young people. Every day, the curiosity from colleagues and from new interns continued. Every day, I was continuously marked as someone who was different in the office. But not different in a negative way. Different in a way that marked me as someone who people trusted. I was marked as someone who, although I continued to be an under-sharer, when I did share, people stopped to listen. What was supposed to be a six-month post-graduated fellowship, turned into four and a half years moving from legal fellow, to staff attorney, and finally to the interim director of the project. This is grace. God's unmerited favor, giving me what I did nothing to deserve, so that He could be glorified. When I made the decision to stop hiding my true voice about my faith everything changed. Doors opened. People were impacted. Holiness led me to experience greater dimensions of God.

Color You _____ Moment

<u>Questions to Ponder:</u>

I saw Black Panther in the theater three times. Partially, because it's a great honor to live in a time when Black folks are making an impact by using their voices to tell an important story on the big screen and partially, because the movie was so rich.

After they believed King T'Challa died, Nakia, tech princess and sister to the presumed dead King, tries to convince Okoye, the commander of the King's bodyguards, to flee Wakanda with them and go against the new king. But Okoye tells Nakia: "I am loyal to the throne. What are you loyal to?"

The first time I saw the movie, I thought: "Whoa, her brother just died and you are basically part of their family! How could you say that?" But each time I watched the movie, I realized the depth of Okoye's jealousy for and commitment to protecting the throne, Wakenda, and her people.

Okoye's words and actions are not unlike Phinehas's. What seem like harsh words and actions reflect a life of deep conviction in what it means to be set apart.

- How would you respond to Okoye's question: What are you loyal to?
- What is challenging about living as holy (being set apart as sacred to the Lord as we become more like the Lord)?
- How have you "yoked" or attached yourself to things that aren't God and/or how have you twisted God's truths?
- What does holiness look like for you in the tension between God's promises and their fulfillment?

ENDLESSLY IN WONDER

"Oh, these vast, calm, measureless mountain days, days in whose light everything seems equally divine, opening a thousand windows to show us God." // John Muir

The tension is an adventure of transformation. God leads us through transformative experiences that reveal His wonder. Wonder is an inspiring sense of awe from something inexplicably beautiful. As we behold creation - a sunrise, a city skyline, and a summit view - we behold the wonders of God's creative voice. God created wonder for us to behold through an utterance of His voice. And with you and me, He did so much more than speak. He put His hands on us and breathed His breath into us to create something out of nothing. Often we can accept the wonder of God-spoken structures - those inexplicably beautiful things we behold in creation. But it's much harder for us to accept the wonder in God-touched and God-breathed beings. When we behold God-spoken wonders, they ought to teach us about our inexplicable beauty and inspire us with a sense of awe. This sense of awe starts with us.

How do we accept that we are God-designed to inspire a sense of awe?

How do we accept that we are something inexplicably beautiful? How do we accept that when we behold God's wonders they are powerful enough to transform us into our God-design?

We Become What We Behold

Jumping back into the story, Moses passed away and Joshua became the leader of the Israelites community. Remember, Joshua and Caleb were the two leaders at the beginning of the story who spoke according to the vision of the Promised Land - the land flowing with milk and honey. They encouraged the people to go in and possess the land that God had already given them as a possession. Now, we are about to pass over the Jordan River into the promise. While Caleb isn't explicitly mentioned, we know that God promised that both Joshua and Caleb would enter the promise and Caleb was one of the leaders of the tribe of Judah, so we know that he was there for this pivotal moment.

On the banks of the Jordan River - this vast body of water that separated them from the promise - and the Israelites receive this instruction:

> "As soon as you see the ark of the covenant of the Lord your God being carried by the Levitical priests, then you shall set out from your place and follow it. Yet there shall be a distance between you and it, about 2,000 cubit in length. Do not come near it, in order that you may know the way you shall go, for you have not passed this way before. Then Joshua said to the people, "Consecrate yourselves, for tomorrow the Lord will do wonders among you." [Joshua 3:3-5]

They are on the brink of something wonderful! The first part of the instruction marks a shift. The Ark of the Covenant was a special nuclear box that held reminders of God's promises to the Israelites and mysteriously the presence of God himself. Throughout the wilderness wanderings, the ark was in the center of the Israelite camp. From the center, pillars representing the presence of God would guide them as a cloud by day and fire by night. But now the ark is repositioned to go in front of the people. The shift is moving us towards something wonderful.

The instruction continues, calling the Levitical priests to carry the ark in front of the people. This marks another shift. Generally, when the ark was transported one clan of Levites was assigned to transport the ark. Here, the Levitical priests were called to carry the ark in front of the Israelites. The Israelites beheld the ark and their highest spiritual leaders in going before them leading them towards the expectant wonder coming the next day.

In the tension, we may feel stuck. We may confront the same struggles day after day after day. We may find ourselves stuck in a matrix of circumstances thinking we can't escape. We may buy into a false reality that becomes our true reality. Being stuck in the tension can leave us feeling desensitized and numb.

The Bible doesn't tell us whether the Israelites felt stuck in the tension, but I get the sense in the first part of this instruction that God wanted to shift things and give them a refreshing glimpse of His wonder. In the tension, God will often use an old thing in a new way to lead us towards beholding His wonder. That's what we see God doing here. God takes two realities that the Israelites were very familiar with - the ark and the Levitical priests - and uses these realities in a completely new way. Then they're told to follow the new way when they see it. I can only imagine that after all these years in the tension doing things the same way, this instruction was unexpected. It's often the unexpected that unlocks our sense of awe in what God may be up to next.

What realities in your life is God using in new ways to lead you towards beholding His wonders?

The instruction continues telling the people they should keep a distance between themselves and the ark of approximately 2,000 cubits (roughly 3,000 feet). Throughout the wilderness wanderings, the Israelites grew accustomed to the ark in the middle of the camp. So, when they moved from place to place, the ark remained in the middle of their traveling, not far ahead of them. Now, they're instructed to stay nearly 3/4 of a mile away from the ark. If I'm an Israelite, excited to behold the wonders the Lord is promising, I'm not interested in staying 3/4 of a mile away. I'm interested in leaning forward to get a front row seat to what He's up to ahead of me. And yet, God instructs a space between the ark carried by the Levitical priests and the people.

Why would God give this instruction? They needed the distance. Only through the distance could they see the way God was leading them, because this way was a new way. (By the way, this detail about the way being new to them, makes me think that in their wilderness wanderings, they were just traversing over their same tracks over and over and over again. Before we shake our heads at the Israelites for walking in circles, take a second to realize that we traverse over our same tracks over and over and over again too!) What a new way they were about to see! The Levitical priests carrying the ark walked directly towards and into the Jordan River. This way was new to them and new to the world. No one had walked on a dry path through the Jordan River. People had heroically swam through the Jordan - the two spies Joshua sent into Jericho had to cross the Jordan somehow and it's likely that they swam there and back. But now, all of the Israelites were about to walk through a dry path in the Jordan River. God knew they needed to space to behold the wonderfulness of God's wonder.

As God draws us near to His wonders, He creates a tension within the tension. This space between us and the wonder we're about to enter into is the tension within the tension - we're shifting our perspective to see it as we shift our lives to become immersed in it. The anticipation of the wonder we behold keeps us wondering how we will hold the wonder. If you've ever driven up a summit road to the top of a mountain or hiked up to a summit you can appreciate this tension within the tension. From the bottom of the mountain, you catch glimpses of the wonderful summit off in the distance, but there's a space between you and the summit - a winding road or challenging trail that's not always in full view. The space between is a space that often takes longer to navigate than you expected and comes with challenges and victories all its own. But as you drive or hike, you behold the wonderful summit, knowing that you're drawing nearer and nearer to it, closing the gap of the space between. This is how we navigate the tension within the tension as we behold God's wonders ahead of us. The space between gives us the space to see the way to the wonder. The way the wonder is not a well-tracked path. It's a trackless path where our faith is increased. With every step we take we draw out a deeper faith that we will reach the wonder. This is how we become what we behold.

As our eyes are fixed on something awe-inspiring and inexplicably beautiful, we are shaped by the faith that we will reach the wonder. We are shaped by confidence that His wonders are real - as real as we are. We are shaped by the reality that because His wonders are real, what He says, does, and creates out of us is real too. Beholding the wonders of God call us to the adventure of blazing a new trail. A new trail towards His wondrous reality and a new trail towards our wondrous reality in Him. When you blaze a new trail towards the wonder you behold, the tension of the trail causes you to become what you behold.

There's an important final part of the instruction. Yes, God absolutely wants us to behold His wonders. Yes, we can be certain that as we behold His wonders, we become wondrous. But before beholding and becoming, there's a process of sanctification. Joshua tells the people to consecrate themselves today for the wonders God would do among them tomorrow. The consecration was preparation. Consecration in the Hebrew language of this instruction means a preparation of setting oneself apart as wholly dedicated to the Lord. In the Old Testament, this preparation involved putting on new clothes, washing oneself, ridding one's home of idols, and other ritual practices. As the Israelites engaged in these practices, they reflected that every area of their lives was wholly dedicated to the Lord. The Israelites prepared themselves physically, and the physical became an outward representation of an inward meditation of obedience, repentance, and faith. When Joshua told the people to consecrate themselves, they understood that before they could fully experience and appreciate the wonder, they needed inward preparation. They understood that they had to be all in with and for God to become what they would behold.

We prepare for beholding wonder through consecration. While we don't perform ritual clothes changing, washings, and burning of idols under the new covenant, we learn from these ancient Israelite ritual practices the significance of wholeness in ourselves, so that we can be wholly dedicated to God. Consecration causes us to align our inward desires and outward realities. Often in the tension, our inward desires to live our God-design don't match our outward realities of the day-to-day struggle. When we are misaligned with our God-designed selves, it's harder to shift our perspective to truly behold the fullness of His wonders. When we are misaligned, we think what a pretty sunrise, what a beautiful garden, or what a profound painting, but we fail to understand the larger implications of those wonders. We fail to appreciate that God may be using that God-spoken structure to lead us to see our God-breathed wondrous selves - a self that can be hard to see when we feel stuck in the tension.

Consecration invites us to integrate our faith in every part of our lives. In the same way you would never set out towards hiking to a summit without preparing physically and materially, consecration is how we prepare physically, spiritually, and emotionally for His wonders. If we continue to engage in integrating and aligning our lives - which is consecration to God - then we will continually live endlessly in wonder. Our consecration today, prepares us to behold His wonders in the tension of tomorrow, so that we can fully become what we behold.

We Pass Over Into Who We're Becoming

"So when the people set out from their tents to pass over the Jordan the priests bearing the ark of the covenant before the people, and as soon as those bearing the ark had come as far as the Jordan, and the feet of the priests bearing the ark were dipped in the brink of the water (now the Jordan overflows all its banks throughout the time of harvest) the water coming down from above stood and rose in a heap very far away, at Adam, the city that is beside Zarethan, and those flowing down toward the Sea of Arabah, the Salt Sea, were completely cut off. And the people passed over opposite Jericho. Now the priests bearing the ark of the covenant of the Lord stood firmly on dry ground in the midst of the Jordan,

and all Israel was passing over on dry ground until
all the nation finished passing over the Jordan."
[Joshua 3:14-17]

There are defining moments in Scripture that punctuate the
redemptive work of God in the midst of humanity. This is one of
those moments. The day of wonder arrived. The people of Israel
set out from their encampment in the wilderness to pass over
into who they were becoming. This chosen people who received a
promise from God that they would possess the land flowing with
milk and honey set out towards the Jordan.

Imagine the magnitude of the scene. The Israelites begin to walk
this new way following the Levitical priests and they walk directly
towards the Jordan River. A parenthesis in the middle of this
scene tells us the Jordan River overflows its banks at the time
of the harvest. This parenthesis that we may read over gives
us an important detail. We discover that the Jordan River was
approximately 100 feet wide at this time of year - double its
average width. This is the new way God led them towards! He
led them towards a seemingly non-traversable river.

The Levitical priests stood at the edge of this overflowing and
wide river and as they dipped their feet into the water, God
initiated the wonder. The waters that typically rushed down
were stuck in a heap in a city approximately 30 miles and the
water that ran down towards the sea were cut off. If you're one of
the Levitical priests your standing at the edge of the impossible
believing that the wonders God promised were possible. If you're
an Israelite standing about 3/4 of a mile away from the ark and
you see this from a "zoomed out" perspective, you must be in awe
of what God is doing.

The priests didn't just stand at the edge, they continued to walk with the ark directly into the middle of the Jordan River. When they got to the middle, they stood firmly on dry ground until all of the Israelites passed over onto the opposite side - the side of the Promised Land. These priest were indeed trailblazers. They dared to stand in the deepest part of the Jordan River. They stood where they could be swallowed up completely by the flood of waters if the waters didn't remain cut off. They stood in the middle of a river where it should have been muddy and caused them to sink into the mud because the river was so deep. They stood firmly in that place on dry ground while the Israelites passed over the wonder into who they were becoming.

Just like the Israelites saw the wonder from a distance, we are often given a glimpse of the wonder from a distance before we pass over into who we are becoming. God gives us glimpses of wonder in many ways: a prophetic prayer, a God-dream in our imagination, or even a moment when we do something new that sparks us to truly come alive. These glimpses, at first, will be in the distance, but God uses them to increase our faith. As we behold glimpses of His wonder from far off, we are spurred forward to draw near in confidence towards that prophetic prayer, that God-dream, that God-calling. I imagine as the Israelites got a glimpse of the boldness of the Levitical priests and the miracle of the waters remaining stuck on both sides, it sparked something in them that they hadn't felt while they were stuck in the tension. A glimpse of wonder that got them unstuck. In the tension where we may feel stuck, these glimpses renew our faith, hope, and confidence, so that we become a people ready to possess the promises of God.

Who are your priestly trailblazers that help you catch glimpses of God's wonders? The redemptive work of Christ on the cross teaches us that Christ has become our high priest forever. This means that one of those priestly trailblazer - the ultimate priestly trailblazer - went into the midst of the greatest obstacle we'd ever face - death itself - and overcame the sting of death for those who believe. He stood and stands firm forever in the midst of our Jordan River as the priest and the ark leading us towards the fulfillment of His promises. Not only do we have Christ as our ultimate priestly trailblazer, but also we are a holy and royal priesthood.[49] We are a priesthood of believers. We possess the spiritual authority to minister directly to God and to others. Our brothers and sisters in Christ have the spiritual authority to minister directly to God on behalf of us and to us on behalf of God.

Who are your priestly trailblazers?
Who are the people in your life who carry the ark in front of you?
Who are the people who stand on the edge of wonder for you?
Who are the people who dare to blaze trails towards the new ways that God has for you?
Who are the people who stand firm in the midst of the obstacles that God transforms into wonder for you to pass over into who you're becoming?

In our lives, we need a priesthood of believers whose faith is so daring and firm that they dare to blaze trails and stand firm. As wonderful as wonder is, wonder can also be scary. It's scary, because we are walking towards the new way of the unknown. And even when we catch a glimpse of it, it's not reality until we're in the midst of it passing over into who we're becoming. Since this is a way we've never passed before, there will be moments when we ask: "Is this safe" "Is this really happening?" The reality is that it isn't safe - wonders never are, because faith never is. But it is really happening. The prayer is now a reality. The God-dream is coming to life. The God-calling is tangible. We need priests to go before us, to stand on the edge for us, and to stand firm in the midst for us. We need to know that even though it isn't necessarily safe, we will be okay. On the trackless path towards who we are becoming, we can find strength in the tracks the priestly trailblazer began for us.

But it doesn't end there.

It's both interesting and terrifying to me that the priestly trailblazers only went halfway. Imagine you're the first Israelite who has to continue the trail towards the other side after the tracks the priests left have stopped. (Also, in our lives, we are always that first Israelite who has to continue the trail). While taking that first step may have been terrifying, the priests paced the Israelites, so they would have the momentum to keep going. Your priestly trailblazers will pace you, so you have the momentum to pass over into who you're becoming.

Remember the hike up to the summit. When you hit those trails, never hit them alone. Hike with someone. Hike with someone who will pace you. Someone who helps you climb over boulders and fallen trees. That person or those people will pace you - and you will pace them - so that you can reach the summit. This is what the priests did for the Israelites. They paced them, so when it came time for the first Israelite to take the first step on a trackless path through the dry ground of the Jordan River, they would have the momentum to step with faith, hope, and confidence. You can only pass over into who you're becoming when you have priests who are with you in the wonders of the tension.

The experience of wonder changes us. We can never behold wonder and pass over wonder and leave the same way we came. We become someone new when we pass over wonder. When we experience the inspiring awe of something inexplicably beautiful it transforms the way we behold everything else. Our normal is new. We see normal now in light of the beauty we've beheld. We see ourselves, our potential, and our voice in light of the beauty we've experienced. The Lord brought the Israelites through a trackless path they had never walked before. He brought them through the way of wonder. The inexplicably beautiful reality we experience happens in the midst of the tension.

But the tension wasn't over just because they crossed the Jordan River. God gave them a wonder in the tension, because on the other side of that wonder was Jericho. A fortified city with a powerful king and army. They crossed the Jordan and now they had an entire land they had to possess. And while none of that would be easy, the wonders they beheld and passed over showed them who God was and who they were becoming. Our wonders do the same for us. They show us how wonderful our God is. They show us the new ways of how He creates and commands. They show us the new ways He wants to use us to reveal wonder to the world by revealing how wonderful we are. The God who makes inexplicably beautiful things inspires us with His inexplicably beautiful essence. The new way of wonder inspires us with the truth that as He creates, we can create. As He is wonderful, we are wonderful. As He inspires, we can inspire. The new way of wonder in the tension transforms us into the kind of people who can dispossess anything that is possessing the promises we've been God-designed to possess.

We Speak of How We Became Who We're Becoming

Before the Israelites continue in the tension to dispossess what is possessing God's promise, they mark their victories and obstacles in the wonder. Joshua gives this instruction to twelve Israelite leaders:

"Pass on before the ark of the Lord your God in to the midst of the Jordan, and take up each of you a stone upon his shoulder, according to the number of the tribes of the people of Israel, that this may be a sign among you. When your children ask in a time to come, "What do those stones mean to you?" then you shall tell them that the waters of the Jordan were cut off before the ark of the covenant of the Lord. When it passed over the Jordan the waters of the Jordan were cut off. So these stones shall be to the people of Israel a memorial forever." [Joshua 4:5-7]

There's a classic 90s song by Ace of Base that says: "I saw the sign that opened up my eyes, I saw the sign"? (If you don't, you need to go google it right now for laughs about how cheesy 90s music really was. Alright, now that you've had a good laugh about that classic 90s gem, let's talk about the significance of signs.) Ace of Base was right, signs open up our eyes to see. They help us know which exit to get off of or when to yield for pedestrians at a crosswalk. Signs are significant markers that point us in the direction of significant things. They open up our eyes to what's important. So, in this scene we see how these stones are meant to be a sign. They are meant to be a marker that points to something significant. The stones point to the fulfillment of God's promise to bring them into the Promised Land. They arrived on the other side of what seemed impossible. The promise was no longer something on the other side of the Jordan River. They were standing on the land. On this Promised Land, they set up a marker of God's faithfulness.

Too often we pass over into who we're becoming without speaking of how we became who we're becoming. We probably do this because we are so excited to lean ahead towards the next season, towards the next step, towards possessing the promise. But we need to mark the places of God's faithfulness. We need to mark the land with a sign of who He is and who we are in Him. It's so easy to experience a wonder like miraculously traversing the obstacle of the Jordan River and be pumped up on euphoria. We're all energies to continue forward thinking we're invincible. But remember, they were still in the tension. We are still in the tension. And in the tension, we need the wonders and we need the signs that mark God's faithfulness through the wonders.

Before we take another step forward into possessing the promises, we have to pull the stones from the wonder. These stones can be lessons we learned, details we saw, or inspiration we felt when we were in the midst of the wonder. We take those stones from the midst of the wonder and set them up in the midst of the continuing tension. Pull that lesson that detail, that inspiration out of the wonder and place it as a marker that will point you towards who God is and who you are in God.

There was another set of stones set up as a sign from this wonder. These stones were in the midst of the Jordan River.

> And Joshua set up twelve stones in the midst of the Jordan, in the place where the feet of the priests bearing the Ark of the Covenant had stood; and they are there to this day. [Joshua 4:9]

What a moment this must have been for Joshua. The text doesn't tell us whether he set up these stones on his own while the priests continued to stand firm or whether he had buddies helping him. I like to imagine him on his own - just him, the Lord, and the priests standing firm holding the Ark of the Covenant in place. This man, like Caleb, held onto faith all those years ago when the majority let go. He was tenacious in the tension and now he is the leader who brought them through the greatest obstacle between them and the promise. We find out later that God exalted him above the people and they stood in awe of him - they stood in wonder of him. The extraordinary reality about the wonders of God is that they teach us to speak of how we became who we are becoming. I like to think that Joshua - in a moment away from everyone - stood in the midst of the wonder knowing that the Lord is truly wonderful, and he was truly wonderful.

These stones that Joshua set up in the midst of Jordan River were a sign of the miracle of God's wonders. The placement of this marker was meant to remind them of the perpetual presence of the Lord in the midst of their greatest tensions. Interestingly, Joshua sets up twelve stones. The number twelve in the Bible is one of the perfect numbers signifying God's power and authority over foundations and structures. This significance reminds us that even in the midst of our obstacles in the tension, God is powerful and sovereign to establish the foundations of His perfect authority. Joshua sets up these stones as a sign that was visible even when the waters receded back to their normal flow in the Jordan River. Scholars speculate on what this actually meant. Some suppose that the stones were large boulders that could be seen above the waters even during the peak harvest season. Some suppose that because the waters of the Jordan are said to be clear you could see the stones set up through the waters. In any event, this marker in the midst of the river that could be seen, was a beautiful reminder of the miracle of God's wonder. The obstacle that seemed non-traversable and yet God in His power and authority transformed it into a wonder that the people of Israel and Joshua beheld and became.

As we go through the tension and experience God's wonders we cannot lean ahead until we, like Joshua, take a reflective moment of our own in the midst of the wonder and mark the wonder.

When we mark the places of God's wonders, we acknowledge the authority of God over the tension. We acknowledge his sovereignty over our lives and over His design of our lives. We acknowledge that we are wonderfully made in him. We speak of how we became who we're becoming. When you behold something awe-inspiring and inexplicably beautiful you are marked. You can never leave that wonder the same way you came into it. We mark the wonders, so that we can fully embrace the transformative work the wonder has performed in us and will perform through us. Mark the wonders. Mark the transformation. Mark the wonder you became.

The View Behind You

Jamaica Pond is a pond in Boston that jumpstarted my spiritual discipline of running. I grew up playing soccer, but from college through the bar exam, I was on an exercise hiatus. And then one day I realized that my sedentary lifestyle wasn't really adding to my life. So, I started running. For three years, I ran Jamaica Pond in the same direction 2-4 times a week. Until one day, as I took a step in my normal direction, I felt this impression in me telling me to run the other way. I didn't doubt it. I didn't question it. I ran with it. Literally.

My friend took a photography class once and the teacher told the class that often times the best views are the views behind you. That statement rang in my head as I made my way around the Pond. I saw the best views of the trees, foliage, viewpoints, and terrain. Views that are normally behind me. As I ran, I was in awe of the beauty of the landscape and I was proud of the terrain that I never realized I climbed. In many ways, running the other way felt like running around a new pond.

I knew God was up to something. I knew the impression I felt was Him telling me to run the other way. But in the moment, I didn't have a full picture of His intention that day or even in the days that followed.

About two weeks later, I stood in church singing and praying during the worship set and a friend came to pray for me. She started describing feelings of weakness and exhaustion that I was feeling, but hadn't uttered out loud. She described how I felt like I didn't have the strength to continue forward. All of these true feelings described how I was doing in the midst of my own tension between God's promises and their fulfillment.

Then she said: "but we can look backwards and see how You've brought her to this place through other moments of feeling weak with no strength to keep going forward."

In that moment, God brought into my mind the impression that I felt that prompted me to run the other way - to look backwards. I saw myself running the other way and realizing the amazing views that were behind me on every run for three years. Then, I saw myself running the other way in my life and remembering the amazing views behind me. The beautiful landscapes of God's faithfulness. The wonderful victories over challenging terrains. The wonders that I beheld and became.

There's clarity in looking back and marking the wonders. When we look back, we take the time to run the other way and see the great views behind us. Looking backwards helps us look forward with clarity. We see that God's intentions towards us and for us have never changed. We trace the terrain of His faithfulness. We track the steps of the victories. We discover ourselves in His greater story of redemption and restoration. We recover the truth of our transformation - which we have been transformed, we are being transformed, and we will be transformed. We run the other way to remember and mark the wonder of who God is and who we are becoming.

My friend continued to pray that based on looking backwards, we can look forward knowing there is strength for this season. In my mind, I could see myself running in my "normal" direction around the Pond with a renewed sense of enthusiasm knowing what was behind me. I could see the race of my life - still in the tension - with a sense of endless wonder.

As I looked back at the markers of the obstacles and victories, I had a renewed perspective for how to run forward. Reflecting over the wonders that I had beheld in my life and how those wonders transformed me into who I'm becoming, clarified God's intentions for me. His intentions for me to not give up. His intentions for me to keep running. His intentions for me to continue to be tenacious in the tension.

God has called you to run towards a vision He has already given you. He's promised you something that's already yours. He's promised me something that's already mine. When we take the time to look backwards and mark the wonders, we get a clearer view of His intention for us as we run forward.

The next time I went for a run around Jamaica Pond, I ran in my "normal" direction. This time, I ran thinking of the great wonders behind me. And guess what? I ran faster than my average pace per mile. I ran stronger and steadier than I had ever run.

Color You _____ Moment

Coloring Exercise: Moments of Wonder

In this chapter of our journey, I mentioned this important truth:

> Before we take another step forward into possessing the
> promises, we have to pull the stones from the wonder. These
> stones can be lessons we learned, details we saw, or inspiration
> we felt when we were in the midst of the wonder. We take
> those stones from the midst of the wonder and set them up
> in the midst of the continuing tension. Pull that lesson that
> detail, that inspiration out of the wonder and place it as a
> marker that will point you towards who God is and who you
> are in God.

I've learned that often times, we are drawn to our God-designed
colors before we become our God-designed color. God's wonders
often reveal our inexplicable beauty to us through images or objects
that catch our eye and teach us about God. As we are learning
about God, He's teaching us about ourselves. We discover the
images or objects create a color palette that's not only reflecting
God, but also reflecting our color and our voice.

When we began our journey, I shared this with you:

> Color me yellow.
> Yellow, the way this color mixes with other colors to create
> new shades, tones, and hues.
> Yellow, the way a bright yellow umbrella provides shelter from
> the rain.
> Yellow, the way bright yellow rain boots scamper through
> Spring's rain puddles.
> Yellow, the way rays break through a cloud-filled day.

Yellow, the way light beams from a lighthouse as a beacon of hope for others to find their way.

Yellow, the way the sun breaks through every inch of darkness. Color me a shade that lights the path for others who are searching to express their color.

Color me yellow.

Each of these lines comes from a moment when I beheld God's wonders. God taught me more about Himself and taught me more about myself. Now it's your turn!

- Write down 8-10 moments in your life when you beheld God's wonders.
- For each moment: What were the thoughts and feelings that you experienced as you saw God's wonders?
- For each moment: What lessons, details, and/or inspirations have God's wonders taught you about God? About yourself?
- As you reflect on these moments, what were the inexplicably beautiful images or objects that caught your attention?
- Why did those images or objects resonate with you?
- What color palette do you see emerging from the images or objects that caught your attention?

GIVE ME THIS MOUNTAIN

"Because in the end you won't remember, the time you spent working in the office or mowing the lawn. Climb the mountain." // Jack Kerouac

You cannot fully possess what you do not fully inhabit. For seven years after Joshua and the Israelites wondrously walked through the dry ground of the Jordan River into the Promised Land, they conquered cities, kingdoms, and regions. However, even with a lot of land conquered over many years, the Lord tells Joshua that there remained "very much land to possess."[50] With this reality, the time came to divide the land among the tribes as an inheritance. The first allotment of land went to Caleb and the tribe of Judah. In this ancient culture, the firstborn child was the first to receive the inheritance. While Caleb and the tribe of Judah were not the firstborn tribe of Israel, his faith when Moses sent the twelve into the land to explore it and his tenacity in the tension of the wilderness gave him the rights of the firstborn.

Jumping back into the story, we meet the Israelites at Gilgal. In Gilgal, the Israelites established a pillar of stones to remind them of God's faithfulness to bring them into the promise. Although the Lord did bring them into the promise, the Israelites spent seven years camping in Gilgal. They continued to live as nomads in the Promised Land. But now Caleb's voice resonates in the scene and he asks for the land the Lord gave him forty-five years earlier, almost to say: "I no longer want to live as a nomad in the land I was promised to inhabit." He understood that even though they conquered a lot of the land, you can't fully possess what you don't fully inhabit. The Lord promised him a specific inheritance of that land. But inheritance requires inhabitance. Inhabitance is full possession. Full possession requires specifically dispossessing what possesses the promise, so that promise can be fully inhabited. Inhabitance is permanent possession of the promises of God. But this means war.

I have a confession. When I saw the wonder of the Jordan River happen, I really wanted that to be the end of the tension. I wanted that to be the end of the story. It's what makes sense, right?

The Israelites behold this wonder. They're transformed into who they're becoming and they're in the Promised Land. Bam! This should have been the end of the tension. This should have been the fulfillment of God's promises. They should have found their voice already! But you can't fully possess what you don't fully inhabit. And while they were in the land, they were camping in it like nomads, not living in it like inhabitants.

The reason the tension doesn't end is because being in the promise, doesn't mean possessing the promise. Some of us never fully possess the promises of God for our lives, because we're too comfortable camping in the places we were called to inhabit. Camping allows us the flexibility to pack up and leave quickly when things get hard; inhabiting commits us to staying through good and bad seasons. When you camp you don't have the intention to stay long-term, because it's a short-term mentality. Inhabiting somewhere has long-term implications, because it requires you to see beyond what's immediate. For these Israelites who spent 47 years camping, they had no understanding of the permanence of inhabitance. In fact, they weren't supposed to have an understanding of this. In the wilderness, they were supposed to be camping nomads, because the wilderness was not meant to be their dwelling place. But that season was over. Now was the season for inhabitance. But what is often scary about this part of the tension is that to inhabit a promise, we have to go to war with something that is adversely possessing God's promise.

When the Lord makes a promise to you, His desire is not simply that you make your presence known. His desire is that you inhabit the promise. So how do we do it? How do we go to war to fully dispossess what possesses our promises, so that we can fully inhabit them? Caleb's actions will give us insight into answering this question. But before we trace his actions, we need to understand the type of war we enter into in the tension. The reality and characteristics of our war are very different from Caleb's war. Our war in the tension is not physical, but spiritual.

> "For though we walk in the flesh, we are not waging war according to the flesh. For the weapons of our warfare are not of the flesh but have divine power to destroy strongholds. We destroy arguments and every lofty opinion raised against the knowledge of God, and take every thought captive to obey Christ" [2 Corinthians 10:3-5]

Our war is a spiritual one, not a fleshly warfare using earthly weapons. We don't fight with our talents, wealth, eloquent arguments, or feelings. We fight with the spiritual armor of God's Kingdom. We put on the full armor of God and we stand firm with the belt of truth, the breastplate of righteousness, the boots of peace, the shield of faith, the helmet of salvation, and the sword of the Spirit, which is the word of God.[51] These spiritual weapons give us the spirit-filled power to destroy obstacles that are opposed to God's truth. We dispossess these obstacles by speaking words aligned with the truths of God revealed to us through the Holy Spirit. We overthrow human-crafted opinions, theories, presumptions, and feelings that go against the revealed truth of God. We speak with the voice of God's Spirit in us, we subdue faulty voices that elevate themselves above His voice. We bring those faulty voices into compliance with the voice of God's truth.

> "For we do not wrestle against flesh and blood, but against the rulers, against the authorities, against the cosmic powers over this present darkness, against the spiritual forces of evil in the heavenly places." [Ephesians 6:12]

We simultaneously dwell in a physical and spiritual realm. Our warfare happens in the spiritual realm. And that warfare directly impacts the physical realm. Evil is real. Sin is real. Darkness is real. But goodness, righteousness, and lightness are both real and the truths of God's Kingdom that cannot be overcome. We use these truths to wage war against the evil, sin, and darkness in the spiritual realm inside of us, in others, and all around us. Our war in the tension is against giant fears, lies, flaws, and wounds that stand in the places of God's promises. So, to fully possess God's promises, we must dispossess those fears, lies, flaws, and wounds. Let's go to war.

My Great War

I was three years old when I decided I wanted to be judge. Yes, you read that correctly, three years old. What did I know? My dad had us on a steady diet of a classic 1980s television show: *Night Court*. *Night Court* was a hilarious sitcom set in a criminal court room during the night shift with an unorthodox and sarcastic judge. I wanted to be a judge like that. It wasn't until later on when someone told me that if I wanted to be a judge, I needed to become a lawyer first. Challenge accepted. The more I learned about lawyers, the more I wanted to become a lawyer. This was the dream.

In the middle of 2014 (after three years of living that dream), the Lord started to stir my heart towards full-time ministry. I became convinced that this was not real and an odd distraction. We had a dream. We had a plan. I went to law school. I fought with the bar exam three times before passing it. We're living the dream. God, what are these thoughts and impressions you're planting in me? What are you inviting me towards?

Truthfully, it scared me. God didn't scare me. My giant fears about the implications of these impressions scared me. I feared surrendering my dreams. I feared the financial uncertainties. I feared the loss of a title. I feared the pressures of full-time ministry. I feared admitting the truths God was revealing to me to anyone. I feared explaining to everyone in my life what God was promising me. I was afraid. Fear is a lie that we choose to believe as a truth. As I overanalyzed all of the lies I told myself about the Lord's radical invitation to full-time ministry, I allowed the lies to become truths I believed. I was afraid.

Then one day papa called. I was twenty-eight years old at the time and I'm one of those kids who calls their parents nearly every single day. They're not just my parents. They're my pastors, my mentors, my friends, and my home. When I saw papa's name on my caller ID, I thought something was wrong. He never calls. I answered the phone and he told me he needed to apologize to me about something. I had no clue what he was talking about. He told me he knew the calling and the promises God had for my life - to use me in full-time ministry. But he was scared and he had been fighting God for a while. He asked God why He wouldn't just let me be a lawyer. He told God he didn't want me to suffer the hardships of ministry. He begged God to let it be another way. Papa told me that throughout the whole night he wrestled with God. (Later my mom would tell me that he wrestled through tears and pain that kept her up through the night, but she had no idea what was happening). Finally, he knew he could not go against the promises of God for my life. He let go of fighting. He let go of holding so tightly to me. He apologized to me for not supporting what God wanted to do in and through my life. He told me that he supported me and that he trusted God's promises and plans.

I was silenced. I was grateful to know papa and I wrestled with the same fears. I was humbled to know that my papa loves me so much that he would wrestle with God for my safety. I was shocked to know that God was confirming His promises for me in papa in such a vivid way. But to be honest, it didn't erase my fears about this radical invitation the Lord was calling me towards. This invitation to die to everything I thought about my life and future. To trust him with who, how, and for what He designed me. I continued to wrestle with my own giant fears in prayer with God.

About a month after my conversation with papa, I received a call from my brother on a Friday evening during Bible Study with my young people. Another rare phone call, so I knew it was important. "They took Pop to the hospital."

My father's health had been declining for years and the doctors could never give us a clear answer about what was wrong. I knew things were bad by the sound of my brother's voice. I knew he had been in incredible pain - not able to walk, swollen, struggling to breathe, and suffering. The weight of this reality interrupted everything.

I waited for the prognosis and the call to get on a plane to come home. A couple of days later, my brother picked me up from the airport. We went straight to the hospital to see papa. He greeted me with the same humor and love as he always did, but he looked so tired and worn. I would spend the next 10 days in the hospital, mostly doing the night shifts with papa. Watching over him through sleepless nights of agony and medicine-induced anxiety. Listening to his weeping and cries out to God in the middle of the night. "What am I going to do?" "What am I going to do, Sarita?" All the while, I was fearfully thinking: "What are we going to do without you?" He was facing a perfect storm of a respiratory infection, kidney failure, bed sores, and only God knows what else.

Then he started to get better. The doctor's advised us to look into a rehabilitation center to move him into the day after Thanksgiving. Things were looking up and I was set to leave Florida on Thanksgiving Day. When I said good bye to papa the night before I left, He was truly content that I was going back. I felt like I could peacefully return back to Boston.

My brother dropped me off at the airport and after I went through security, I saw a text from my mom: "Don't get on the plane."

Papa had stopped breathing and they had to revive him - crash cart and everything like something out of Grey's Anatomy. He was in the ICU…again. I was terrified.

I have no idea how, but I got on the plane. I had a layover in Washington D.C. and I sat in that airport sick to my stomach and crying. God kept replaying Psalm 23 in my head: "Even though

I walk through the valley of the shadow of death I will fear no evil." I knew God was storing those words in my heart, so that they would be the truths waging war against my fears on that Thanksgiving Day.

When I finally arrived in Boston, I spent Thanksgiving Day with a family who is like family to me. I mostly stayed in bed. Exhausted. I waited to hear news about papa and waited to hear when I needed to come back home.

Two days later, on a frigid Saturday evening, I sat in Starbucks working on my sermon for the following day (do not ask me how I continued to minister through this season, but sharing God's word led me to a peace in the midst of the raging fears inside me). Mom called. She told me the doctor's told her we needed to make a decision about keeping him on the tubes that were keeping him alive. I knew, she knew, and my brother knew that papa didn't want to live this way.

I booked a flight for the next day. After preaching, I headed home. We arrived at the hospital late that night. When I walked into the room and looked at papa's eyes, he knew why I had come back.

He was in so much pain, we could only touch him on his head. The tubes in his mouth didn't allow him to talk. But papa always spoke more with his eyes than his words. My brother and I stayed at the hospital for a while until mom told us to go home and get some sleep.

December 8, 2014. The next day. Papa had been in the hospital for nearly a month. We talked to the doctor and agreed that at 5:00PM they could come and remove the tubes. Throughout the day, papa gave us instructions about bills to pay and where to find important documents. Only he would be telling us these things on his last day. He spoke to each of us - in the ways he could. He asked mom and my brother to do certain things. But for me he made no asks, he just told me to go back to Boston. He saw me and understood my fears. He could've asked me to come home. He could've asked me to move back and be there for mom and my brother. He could've asked me to take care of everyone. And He knew I would've done it. But instead he gave me an instruction: go back.

5:00PM. They sent us into the waiting room while they took out the tubes.

We were surrounded in the waiting room by our family and our church family. I'm not even sure how they knew we would need all of them at that specific time. We hadn't had time to reach out and tell anyone. But people kept showing up.

We went back into papa's room and the room was filled with family. Mama stood on the right side of the bed. My brother was on the left closest to papa and I stood next to him. I have no idea how she found the strength, but mama started to sing these old coritos (Spanish songs - kind of like hymns, but so much better!). Papa looked up at her with his eyes lit up. He started singing along with her with his eyes. The whole room following their lead. We sang along with them.

About 45 minutes later, papa was gone.

We wouldn't have been able to leave the hospital without the help of a beloved couple who spiritually carried us out of the hospital. It was their wedding anniversary and they were caring for and carrying us out of the hardest day of our lives. They took us to dinner. They ordered half the menu. We didn't eat much. They took care of us and made it possible for us to take those first steps into our new normal. When we got home, mama paused at every room in our house. To this day, his presence and prayers feel embedded into the walls.

Truthfully, the months that followed are still a blur. I know I went back to work and church, but I can't recall anything from those months. And then six months later, God reminded me that before papa left us I was wrestling with His radical invitation to go into full-time ministry. I started to feel the stirrings again. But, I was living in a new normal. Life looked and felt different. Honestly, I had new fears about the visions God planted in me. I felt like what happened to papa changed everything. It did change our normal, but it didn't change God or His promises. And in this new normal, with the new fears, I also was developing and discovering a deeper faith. I knew I needed to get in the wrestling ring about these promises. War wasn't over. I spent that summer in prayer dispossessing the giant fears that possessed the promises of God for my life.

The fears felt more like giants now than they did in the months before papa left us. I felt more inadequate to go to war than I did before. I felt weaker. I felt more worn. I felt more worried. I felt more afraid. This would be the first major life decision I would make without the counsel and perspective of my father. My father who taught me to live according to the principles of God's framework. My father who modeled living a life of true holiness - set apart by God for God. My father who led me as a priestly trailblazer crossing the Jordan Rivers of my life to behold God's wonders. Papa was with me in every tension of my life - teaching me to be still and know that God is God. And he was gone. And he left unexpectedly in the middle of this tension. Now his agonized question in the deep of night, "What am I going to do?" became my great question before the Lord. What am I going to do about my finances? What am I going to do about my legal profession? What am I going to explain to people? What am I going to do if this doesn't work out the way I think it's supposed to? What am I? What am I? What am I?

These questions became so loud in my head they were battling themselves and crippling me. And then out of nowhere - although in retrospect I think God was trying to shut me up - a job opportunity opened for me to become a coordinator of a youth ministry leadership program coming to Boston. This position seemed perfect. It was a part-time job that would allow me to do leadership development. At the same time, I could continue at my church as a part-time youth pastor. It all seemed perfect. I submitted the application, my resume, and my cover letter. I had great references. I had my whole game plan figured out. I would work at my lawyer job until August 31, 2015, I'd take a month vacation, and then I'd start in October. Everything was going great. I felt peace about this radical invitation to go into full-time ministry. I was one of two finalists for the position. My phone rang with the news. They chose the other person.

Are you kidding me right now, God? I thought this was it! What are you doing to me? This position came out of nowhere, God. Clearly, this must have been you. Right? Distraught and discouraged, the giant fears started to battle loudly in my head again. They had quieted, but they had not gone away. Maybe this was a sign I really shouldn't leave my lawyer job. I started to fear the timing was all wrong. And then I was confronted by this truth: Fear focuses on me and faith focuses on God. My "What am I going to do?" questions and my "perfect game plan" made God's radical invitation about me following me and not about me following God. I couldn't be faithful to God if I was being faithful to my fears. I couldn't go to war with the giant fears, because I was fighting on their side and not against them.

I wished and wondered what my father would tell me to do. I remembered what I told my brother in the hospital just after papa left us. I told him: "You got this." A few days later, we had a conversation, where I shared with him something one of my friends said to me. She said that everything that papa was supposed to teach me, he taught me. My brother and I talked about that truth more specifically as it related to him. We talked about everything from how to buy a house to how to be a dad. That conversation flashed into my mind as I wondered what papa would tell me to do. I recognized that he taught me how to go to war with giant fears every time he taught God's word, every time he trusted God's calling despite people's criticism, and every time he sat in his rocking chair at his little white table balancing the checkbook, so that our family would faithfully steward our finances and there would never be lack in our financial storehouses. He taught me through his life that faith focuses on God not on fear. He taught me how to fix my eyes on the author and perfecter of my faith. He taught me how to go to war against my giant fears, so that I could dispossess them and possess the promises of God.

My mom and I talked about my feelings and fears about the rejection from this position. Hers is the voice that brings clarity to confusion for me and my brother. She helped me to see that if nothing else this experience caused me to put an end date on working at my lawyer job. She helped me to see that the date marked on the calendar was an offensive move towards God's radical invitation. She guided me towards the wisdom of God's truth and God's immovable word. I began to see that this offensive move was not something I should erase from my calendar because my game plan did not go as planned. When someone extends an invitation to you, you set a date with them. The date is a commitment. August 31, 2015 was the date God and I marked in our spiritual calendar.

My next offensive move was to submit my letter of resignation. I had never resigned from anything and the implications of this felt huge. I need all the spiritual weapons I could get, so I decided to fast. I asked that same friend who reminded me that my dad taught me everything he was supposed to teach me to fast with me. Together, we came up with this 7-day fasting and prayer plan[52]:

Day 1: Silencing The Noise
Before we can focus on any of our other prayers, we need to begin by silencing the noise and having that as our foundation. Getting rid of the noise, and the distractions will cause our mind and heart to be in the right place as we go on our week praying for everything else.

Day 2: It's Not About Me
As a second foundational level, once we've quieted our brain and prepared our heart to listen to the Holy Spirit, we need to remind our soul about our place in the midst of all these prayers. This way our heart can have the right posture as we go on throughout the week.

Day 3: Living in the Pool of Promises Instead of Outside the Pool
Once we have our heart in the right posture, we should have our heart in the right mindset and focusing in on those promises and praying our prayers from that place will be more powerful.

Day 4: Peace With My Radical Invitation
Before we can pray for fear to be a catalyst, we should pray about having peace in our soul and comfort with our radical invitation.

Day 5: Fear as a Catalyst not a Paralysis
Once we have quieted our mind, we have our heart in the right posture and mindset, and we have our soul in a peaceful place, we can pray for that spark to launch us into our potential and the moment we were created to live.

Day 6 & 7: The BOLD and BIG Prayer
These prayers are missing something: they're missing the bold and big prayer. They're missing our ask of the impossible and our ask of seeing God's power. While we need help from Him in all of these prayers, they are also things that to a certain degree we can accomplish ourselves. If we actually wanted to, we could silence the noise. We could constantly remind ourselves of our place. We could constantly remind ourselves of His promises and actually trust in them. We could find our own peace and rest. We could take control of our fear. We could do all these things. So, we're missing something.

For the last two days, after we've asked Him for things that we should always be asking Him for anyways, we can take a deep breath in and actually let out what our ask is. It's not our responsibility to see how God will answer, but we owe it to him to let him in on every detail of this ask. The detail we're hoping for is the miracle. Once we've prayed for everything that we needed to pray for, we need to end in the highest of surrenders and ask of Him our deepest desire. Our desire that at the end of all of this - once we've put our foot in the Jordan River - that it actually opens up.

That you have a full time position in ministry. We should end with that ask, with the miracle, with the impossible and with the one thing that totally leaves the results of all of our prayers completely in His hands and not ours.

During the seven days of prayer and fasting, I went to war with every giant fear that possessed my promise. Each day I listened to Elevation Worship's "Your Promises" and declared that it didn't matter what I felt or what I saw, my hope would always be His promises to me. Every day the giant fears became smaller and my giant faith became bigger. The truth of God dismantled my fears and made my feelings obedient to God. I was ready to make the offensive move of resigning from my position out of the overflow of this war waged in the spiritual realm.

When I spoke to my executive director about my resignation, I knew that it came out of left field to him. I had not shared anything about what God was stirring in me and revealing to me with any of my colleagues. I had been completely private about this and he was shocked. In the three weeks that followed, I began to wind-down my role with meetings and a plan for the next director of the project. I felt at peace. I had stewarded this opportunity well, I had learned so much, and I had grown so much from intern, to legal fellow, to staff attorney, to project director. I experienced a new peace. I was heading into the unknown, but the giant fears were dispossessed and I was possessing God's promises for my life.

Looking back at that decision and turning point in my life, nothing went the way I thought it would. More wars have been and continue to be waged. More giant fears, lies, flaws, and wounds have been dispossessed from the promise. I've learned and I'm learning to live out a faith that focuses on God. I've realized that the territory of God's promise for me is wider and vaster than I imagined. There are a lot of giants on this land that need to be disposed. And battling these giants, has allowed God to refine my voice in ways that I didn't even know I needed. The war in this tension goes on.

The promises of God may seem ridiculous. The invitation to possess the promise is radical. You may have some very, very giant fears, lies, flaws, and wounds standing on top of God's promises. Your possession of God's promise in the tension may be unexpectedly interrupted by a tragedy or loss that catapults you in ways you don't fully understand. It is likely that the war is deeper and wider than you anticipate. But as we turn to Caleb's story, his actions give us guidance as to how we go to war to fully dispossess what possesses our promises, so that we can fully inhabit them. God honors our tenacity in the tension. Let's go to war.

Assert (and Reassert) the Promise

> "And Caleb the son of Jephunneh the Kenizzite said to him [Joshua], "You know what the Lord said to Moses the man of God in Kadesh-barnea concerning you and me. I was forty years old when Moses the servant of the Lord sent me from Kadesh-barnea to spy out the land, and I brought him word again as it was in my heart. But my brothers who went up with me made the heart of the people melt; yet I wholly followed the Lord my God. And Moses swore on that day, saying, Surely the land on which your foot has trodden shall be an inheritance for you and your children forever, because you have wholly followed the Lord my God." [Joshua 14:6b-9]

At the beginning of our journey together, we talked how "remembering" is a key instruction in the book of Deuteronomy. The Hebrew word for remember is "zakar" meaning to bring past events to mind so that they impact present feelings, thoughts, and actions. We talked about how as we seek to find our voice in the tension between God's promises and their fulfillment, there would be moments when we would need to "zakar". This is what Caleb does as he moves towards fully dispossessing what possesses God's promise to him.

Sometimes when I read the opening lines of these verses, I hear a bit of sassiness in Caleb's voice: "You *know* what the Lord said..." And for a moment I think: "Bro, be chill... you will get your inheritance. Joshua is planning on dividing the land." But then I take a step back and I realize that Caleb isn't being sassy, he's being assertive about the promises that God made to him 45 years earlier. Assertive means having a confident or forceful personality. In other words, assertiveness is synonymous with boldness, decisiveness, or even self-possessed. When Caleb went to war in the tension for the promise the Lord vowed to him, his voice was assertive. Caleb clearly asserted the promise according to the reality of the experience that he had with the Lord. His voice was self-possessed. The self-possession of Caleb's voice empowered him to begin to dispossess what possessed his promise.

We need to assert our voices about the promises of God. We need self-possessed voices that can dispossess the giants that stand on or against our promises. Like Caleb, our experiences with the Lord give birth to the promises of the Lord over our lives. The reason that we need to remember those experiences is for moments like this. Moments when asserting the experience and the promise will empower us to fully inhabit the promise.

Here's a truth you need to hold on to: The experiences you've had with the Lord where He has revealed promises to you were real. When we are in the tension confronting obstacles, it becomes easier to allow the giant fears, lies, flaws, and wounds to become our faulty truths. The light of hope that once fueled our tenacity in the tension starts to dim and the darkness takes over. The darkness pushes us into a corner where the assertiveness of our voice can become either a faint whisper or a deafening silence. When you begin to doubt the truth of your experiences and God's promises to you here's an important truth:

> "But we have this treasure in jars of clay, to show the surpassing power belongs to God and not to us. We are afflicted in every way, but not crushed; perplexed, but not driven to despair; persecuted, but not forsaken; struck down, but not destroyed; always carrying in the body the death of Jesus, so that the life of Jesus may also be manifested in our bodies. For we who live are always being given over to death for Jesus' sake, so that the life of Jesus also may be manifested in our mortal flesh. So death is at work in us, but life in you.
>
> Since we have the same spirit of faith according to what has been written, "I believed, and so I spoke," we also believe and so we also speak, knowing that he who raised the Lord Jesus will raise us also with Jesus and bring us with you into his presence. For it is all for your sake, so that as grace extends to more and more people it may increase thanksgiving, to the glory of God.
>
> So we do not lose heart. Though our outer self is wasting away, our inner self is being renewed

day by day. For this light momentary affliction is preparing for us an eternal weight of glory beyond all comparison, as we look not to the things that are seen but to the thing that are unseen. For the things that are seen are transient, but the things that are unseen are eternal." [2 Corinthians 4:7-18]

There's so much in these verses and I encourage you to meditate on how God wants to use these words to comfort and confront you. Even though the Apostle Paul wrote these words hundreds of years after Caleb asserted the promise of God in his life, I can imagine Caleb speaking these words throughout the tension. Caleb asserted the promise God made to him even though he lived through very dark moments of despair. He never allowed the light of hope to go dim. He asserted the promise as someone who consistently spoke according to what he believed. Caleb was more focused on the unseen truths of God than the seen giant fears, lies, flaws, and wounds. Caleb spoke knowing that his experiences with God and the promises of God were real and true.

His assertiveness was not arrogance. His assertiveness was grounded in the unseen truths of eternity engraved in his heart by his Creator. I pray that we would have this kind of assertiveness, friends. I pray that the assertiveness of your voice would be grounded in the unseen truths of eternity engraved in your heart by your Creator. We can assert the promise of God when the promise is consistent with the word spoken about us, over us, and out of us. Caleb was assertive with Joshua in that moment, because Joshua heard Moses declare the promise over Caleb's life. Joshua knew that Caleb was affirming the promise he guarded in his heart for 45 years. God's promises are eternally true, because they are consistent from him to us, from others to us, and from us back to others and him.

The other reason Caleb's assertiveness was not arrogance was because of the premise for the promise. The promise was based on the fact that Caleb "wholly followed the Lord." This phrase is mentioned three times - twice from Caleb himself and once about Caleb. Dr. Charles Dodd, a Welsh Biblical Scholar, explains that the Hebrew phrase for "wholly followed the Lord" is *milleeti acharei Jehovah*, (literally meaning, *I filled after the Lord my God*) "give(s) the idea of a traveller, who, attentive to the following of his guide, so treads in his steps, as to leave hardly any void space between his guide and him, and continually fills up the traces of his feet."[53] What a beautiful expression of wholeheartedly following God. This kind of close following is the premise of God's promise for Caleb. Caleb could assert the promise, because he followed the Lord, his guide, so closely that God brought him to this specific place of promise.

Like Caleb, as we go to war in the tension, we need to hold firm to the premise of our promise. We need to wholly follow the Lord without leaving even a little bit of space in between Him and us as we walk to the specific place of his promise. When we go to war to dispossess what possesses the promise of God, we must assert the promise of God with a self-possessed voice that stands firm on the premise of the promise.

Affirm the Values

> "And now, behold, the Lord has kept me alive, just as he said, these forty-five years since the time that the Lord spoke this word to Moses, while Israel walked in the wilderness. And now, behold, I am this day eighty-five years old. I am still as strong today as I was in the day that Moses sent me; my strength now is as my strength was

then, for war and for going and coming." [Joshua
14:10-11]

The mere fact that God has kept you alive until this moment is
proof that He still wants to bring you into the promises He has
for you. Even if it's been forty-five years. Still speaking to Joshua,
Caleb tells him that the Lord had kept him alive for this. The
language used by Caleb here is that he's been living fully alive
throughout all of these years. The Lord empowers us to live
fully alive by knitting his guiding principles into the core of our
God-design. These guiding principles are our core values. Caleb
affirms the values that have sustained and continue to sustain
him through and in the tension towards the promise. Values are
the guiding principles that direct the way you understand and
approach your experiences. Values sustain vitality.

Caleb valued faith, courage, conviction, and devotion. As Caleb
wandered through the wilderness, he maintained faith in the
unseen promise of God for him and his family. In the tension
of the wilderness and even on the other side of the Jordan River,
Caleb retains the courage to continue walking in often trackless
paths. In this honest moment between Caleb and Joshua, we see
the conviction of this eighty-five year old man. I imagine Caleb
with no teeth and all gums, confident about who God is to him
and what God has promised. He's completely devoted to the
Lord who kept him alive, who he has followed, and who he will
continue to follow against the tallest giants and most fortified
cities. Caleb's affirmation sustained his vitality for possessing
the promise.

Why did the Lord keep Caleb alive? Caleb is appointed the
chief of the tribe of Judah.[54] In this capacity, he had the option
to mobilize the many fighting men of Judah to go to war against
the giants and the fortified cities in this hill country. But the Lord

wasn't keeping Caleb alive to appoint others to dispossess what possessed his promise. The Lord kept him alive "for war and for going and coming."[55] Caleb affirms that he was just as strong at 85-years-old as he was when Moses sent him into the Promised Land. The Lord sustained his strength for leading, mobilizing, and advising the tribe of Judah and also for going to war. I love how Caleb's faith, courage, conviction, and devotion sustained him for the purposes of the Lord to be revealed in his life. He was not content living next to or near his promise; Caleb was ready to inhabit the promise. He knew the Lord kept him alive for the purpose of going to war and successfully dispossessing the giants and the fortified cities in Hebron.

Why is the Lord keeping you alive?
What promise is keeping you alive to fully possess by fully inhabiting?

The Lord doesn't keep us alive to stand near His promises while someone else possesses our promises. He's keeping us alive to possess the promises He's made to us. When we, like Caleb, affirm the values God knit into our design, we affirm the purpose of our existence. We affirm the faith that causes us to believe in the unseen truths of our Creator. We affirm the voice of the Lord who calls us to be strong and courageous. We affirm that we stand in the tension with God. We affirm our commitment to loving him with our mind, hearts, souls, and strength, even when it means war.

Ask For the Mountain

The first legal concept I learned in property law was adverse possession. Adverse possession is when someone who is not the landowner possesses the land and their possession may give them ownership rights of the property. The non-landowner must meet five requirements: the possession is 1) continuous, 2) hostile, 3) actual, 4) opens and notorious, and 5) exclusive. During my first semester of law school, adverse possession showed up throughout property, even on my final exam and in my first year writing and research course. By the end of that semester, I had the doctrine of adverse possession and how to apply it pretty engrained into my brain.

When I look at Caleb going into the mountainous region of Hebron and claiming ownership of the land, I start thinking about adverse possession. The Anakites, the giants in the mountains, possessed this land continuously for hundreds of years. The giants weren't just there when Caleb came to explore the land. The giants lived here for years. They built fortified cities with infrastructures, they protected those cities from attacks, and they passed down the land rights as inheritances to their children. All of this, despite the fact that this land was land Abraham purchased hundreds of years earlier.

By all accounts, the Anakites could probably make a strong claim for adverse possession. Legally, it would appear that they could make a claim to this land. At the very least, we may infer that the Anakites were adverse in their possession of the land. Earlier in the book of Joshua, it's mentioned that Joshua and the Israelites drove out the Anakites from this region during their many conquests. However, their continued presence on the land may suggest they returned to repossess the land. We don't know if that was the case. Whether they're back with a vengeance to protect their land or protecting a land that they had never really been drive out of. These giants were not going to go down without a fight. But Caleb asks for the fight.

> "So now give me this hill country of which the
> Lord spoke on that day, for you heard on that day
> how the Anakim were there, with great fortified
> cities. It may be that the Lord will be with me,
> and I shall drive them out just as the Lord said."
> [Joshua 14:12]

"Give me this hill country." Some translations say, "Give me this mountain" and I like the imagery of that. Based on the original language the words "hill country" and "mountain" are both inferred. We don't need to get hung up on semantics, but let's talk geography for a moment, so that we can understand the implications of Caleb's ask.

The city of Hebron was an ancient city about 3,050 feet above sea level within a vast mountainous region of Israel called the Judean Mountains. The Judean Mountain range comprises sub-mountain ranges. One of those sub-mountain ranges are the Hebron Hills. This means that the hill country Caleb asks for is a rocky and complex terrain. We know that Abraham purchased a cave in this region as a burial place for his wife Sarah. (This cave was also the burial place for other members of the patriarchal family.) The presence of one cave, suggests the presence of other caves throughout this hill country. A final feature of this mountainous region is the presence of fortified cities. Fortified cities. Plural. A fortified city in ancient culture was protected by tall stone walls designed to protect a city from attacks of the enemy. Typically, the stone walls were dug deep into the ground, so that they could not be easily knocked down or overcome by attacks. Excavations of the fortified walls of Hebron have found the walls, dating back to the time Abraham and Sarah dwelled there, were approximately 9-ft thick walls.[56]

On these geographical and archeological facts alone, in order to dispossess what possessed Caleb's promise, he asked to traverse not just one mountain, but multiple mountains. He asked to confront enemies who were likely hiding in dark caves. And he asked to overcome multiple cities with thick stone walls protecting them from attacks. Caleb doesn't just ask for one uninhabited city on one mountain. He asked for a whole mountain range with heavily protected cities with giants in them. He asked for a fight.

Caleb's sole dependence for this ask and for this fight was on the Lord and the word the Lord spoke to him about him. We may hear fear or doubt when Caleb says "it may be that the Lord will be with me." But a clearer understanding is Caleb saying: if the Lord will be with me, then I shall possess the Lord's promise to me. Caleb understood that he was 100% dependent on the gracious intervention of the Lord in order to dispossess what possessed his promise. He clearly embraces that the grace of God was fundamental to living out the word of God spoken to him about him. The grace of God covers the word of God. Caleb understood that God's words about Him were covered by God's grace over him.

Caleb's humble boldness exemplifies how we ought to ask for mountains the Lord has promised us. We cannot underplay the boldness of Caleb to ask for this hill country with all of its uncertainty and complexity. But that boldness is perfectly balanced with a humility that recognizes if the Lord isn't with me, then I would never be able to fully inhabit those mountains. We could use a dose of this humble boldness. Often we are under the misconception that the only way to dispossess what possesses our promises is by being humble and patient. Read: By being passive. We pray and say: "God if it's your will blah blah blah." Meanwhile, we disregard the truth that since He promised it in the first place, it IS His will. We've exchanged true humility for a false version of humility where we hold back, so we don't seem prideful.

But Caleb's humility gives a true version of humility that begins with dependence on God. Dependence is our design. We were designed to depend on the sufficiency of God's grace, which is powerful in our weakness. It's with this true humility that we are empowered to ask for the mountains in boldness. Boldness isn't misplaced arrogance; Boldness is rightly placed dependence. It's humble boldness that doesn't ask for God to move the mountain; it asks to possess the mountain.

What if we're wasting too much time praying to have the faith of a mustard seed?
What if we're praying for God to move our mountains and the giants who inhabit them?
What if we're waiting for a response from God?

When really God wants us to possess what is already ours. For many of us we need the humble boldness of Caleb. We need to stop praying for God to move the mountains. We need to start asking for the mountains. We need to fight against the giants in order to dispossess what possesses our promises.

> "According to the commandment of the Lord to Joshua, he gave to Caleb the son of Jephunneh a portion among the people of Judah, Kiriath-arba, that is, Hebron (Arba was the father of Anak). And Caleb drove out from there the three sons of Anak, Sheshai and Ahiman and Talmai, the descendants of Anak." [Joshua 15:13-14]

Go back and read those two verses again. Caleb went to war and drove out the giants. Or in the Hebrew he "yaresh-ed" aka dispossessed what possessed his promise. Let these verses fill you with faith that God will help you find your voice in the tension between His promises and their fulfillment. Let these verses fill you with the truth that the One who brought you to it will bring you through it. He is faithful! He never goes back on His promises! His Word never returns void! And our word in Him is powerful! Alrighty, praise break over for now. Let's talk through this a bit so we can understand some of the implications and applications of this war Caleb fought to fully inhabit the promise.

Kiriath-Arba aka Hebron. I told you earlier we would meditate on the significance of this place. As we ponder upon this hallowed place, it's important to note that when Caleb went to war its name was Kiriath-Arba. Kiriath meaning "city". Arba was the father of Anak and the greatest man among the giants. Kiriath-Arba was the City of Arba. Talk about adverse possession. The Anakim possessing the land named it after a man who was their greatest giant. But, for the Israelites, this place was Hebron.

Here are some Hebron highlights:

-   [Genesis 13:18]: Approximately 3800 years ago, Abraham moved into the Promised Land after the Lord promised him all of the land for him and his offspring and settled in Hebron by the oak trees building an altar there to the Lord.
-   [Genesis 23]: Sarah died in Hebron and Abraham pays an extravagant amount to buy a field and cave from the Ephron the Hittite as a burial place for his wife.
-   [Genesis 35:27-29]: Isaac spent the last years of his life in Hebron and was buried by his sons Jacob and Esau in the cave Abraham bought for Sarah.
-   [Genesis 37:14]: Jacob settled in Hebron with his sons.

- The Cave of Machpelah in Hebron or the Tomb of the Patriarchs is traditionally acknowledged as the burial place of all the patriarchs (Abraham, Isaac, and Jacob) and all the matriarchs (Sarah, Rebekah, and Leah).
- Hebron is one of the most ancient cities in the world.
- Hebron means a community or alliance.

The promise God gave to Caleb forty-five years ago was both significant for Caleb and his story, and significant for God and his bigger story. "Therefore Hebron became the inheritance of Caleb the son of Jephunneh the Kenizzite..."[57] This city was dripping with significance for the people of Israel. The patriarchs of the faith inhabited this hallowed place as an overflow of the promise the Lord gave to Abraham about this land being for him and his descendants. One of those descendants was Caleb as a member of the tribe of Judah. Hebron became Caleb's inheritance. This war Caleb fought for the promise God gave him brought him into communion with an inheritance of the Promised Land. This place was no longer named after a man; this place was renamed after a legacy. A legacy that Caleb inherited.

God's promises to us are specific to our story, but we must never lose sight of the truth that part of being a child of God is being part of a larger story. Caleb wasn't just going to war for something temporal and earthly. He was going to war for something eternal and heavenly. And so it is with us. Finding our voice in the tension between God's promises and their fulfillment is part of a larger story that stretches into an eternal past and an eternal future. This is precisely why we don't wage war against earthly things, but against the principalities in the spiritual dimension. We overcome evil forces in the spiritual realm, because our promises are fulfilled in the spiritual dimension impacting the earthly realm. God wants us to fully inhabit the promises He has for us even more than we want them fulfilled. He knows that when we dispossess what possesses our promises, we then understand the spiritual significance of the promises. Understanding the spiritual significance of God's promises teaches us to embrace the spiritual significance of our voices over giant fears, lies, flaws, and wounds that we go to war with in the tension.

There's another significant dimension to Caleb's passions of Hebron. What did he have to do to possess Hebron?

Here are the two verses again for another praise break, but also so we can read them carefully again:

> "According to the commandment of the Lord to Joshua, he gave to Caleb the son of Jephunneh a portion among the people of Judah, Kiriath-arba, that is, Hebron (Arba was the father of Anak). And Caleb drove out from there the three sons of Anak, Sheshai and Ahiman and Talmai, the descendants of Anak." [Joshua 15:13-14]

Caleb possessed Hebron by dispossessing the three sons of Anak, Sheshai and Ahiman and Talmai. Rewind to the beginning of the story when Caleb, Joshua, and the fearful leaders went into the Promised Land: "They went up into the Negeb and came to Hebron. Ahiman, Sheshai, and Talmai, the descendant of Anak were there."[58] We've heard these three giants' names before. There's no clear evidence about whether or not these three giants are the same giants or whether they are the sons of those giants. But I'm inclined to believe that they are the same giants. If Caleb was still alive after these forty-five years, then who's to say that the giants also weren't still alive. I'm inclined to believe that God likes to see His children overcome the exact giants they are facing and not substitute giants. God had the power to keep these giants vital just like he kept Caleb vital. I won't be offended if you are inclined to believe differently. How significant may it have been for Caleb to dispossess the same giants that possessed his promise? There they were. They were giants known by name. And Caleb would fully inhabit his promise by driving these giants out of the promise. War with these specific giants was what made the promise specific for Caleb.

What are the specific giant fears, lies, flaws, and wounds that possess your promises? God wants us to go to war with the specific giants. As we go to war, God wants our voice secure in the truth of His word to us and over us that we destroy those specific giants. The giant fears, lies, flaws, and wounds are a crucial part of our promises. In fact, I dare to tell you they are a necessary part of our promises. Going to war with our specific giant fears, lies, flaws, and wounds helps us to find our voice in a way nothing else can, because it forces us to speak God's truth over our feelings.

Dispossessing what possesses our promises refines our voice, because we assert God's promises that demonstrate that we stand firm on the premise of the promise. Dispossessing what possesses our promises refines our voice, because we affirm the values that sustain our vitality throughout the tension. Dispossessing what possesses our promises refines our voice, because we ask for the mountain with the giants that reveals our humble boldness.

Color You _____ Moment

Questions to Ponder
- What promise has God given you that you're currently seeking to possess?
- Of your core values, which values are the most relevant to guide you towards possessing God's promise?
- What "giants" possess that promise?

Coloring Exercise: Ask for the Mountain
- Draw the mountain that God has promised to you
- Draw the "giants" that are possessing that mountain
- Draw yourself dispossessing those giants
- Draw yourself on the mountain possessing God's promise

PART 3

BETWEEN GOD'S PROMISES AND THEIR FULFILLMENT

There is more.

As long as we are on this side of eternity, there is more. More promises to possess. More obstacles to overcome and victories to win. More opportunities to strengthen our voices as we discover more of our God-design. The tension, while not an invitation to be tense, but tenacious, can cause weariness. Even when we've won wars, experienced great victories, and seen God fulfill promises, God is still painting an intricately deep masterpiece. There is more.

Do you remember Korah's rebellion when we talked about God's frameworks and Kingdom Principles?

The family of Korah, the Levite, teaches us about the intricately deep masterpiece God is painting. Even though Korah rebelled and experienced the consequences of his rebellion, God, functioning within His framework of love, spares the children of Korah. At the end of the book of Numbers, before the Israelites crossed over into the Promised Land, we discover that "the sons of Korah did not die."[59] And not only did they not die, but God uses the children of Korah for something more.

Samuel, the prophet, who anointed David as King was a son of Korah.[60]
Heman, a singer and King David's seer, was Samuel's grandson and another son of Korah.[61]

The Sons of Korah were chosen by King David to minister with songs at the Tabernacle. They were the original worship pastors. Many of their songs are recorded for us in the book of Psalms. One in particular, teaches us about this Kingdom Principle that there is more: Psalm 42. We won't read the whole Psalm together now, but I encourage you to meditate on this Psalm.

The Sons of Korah seem to understand the heavy and the light of this journey of finding our voice. They seem to understand there are deeper expressions of God and expressions of ourselves. In this song, they speak through the weariness, with a longing for more. We find ourselves in a similar state during this part of our journey to find our voice:

> "Deep calls to deep at the roar of your waterfalls;
> all your breakers and your waves have gone over
> me." [Psalm 42:7]

There are greater depths in you than the ones you've already discovered. We spend our lives discovering a fuller expression of ourselves and a fuller expression of God. It's in this space, the space between, where we find a deeper voice. In between God's promises and their fulfillment, we find a new depth in these fuller expressions. This new depth - where our depths and God's depths are calling out to each other - is a space of strengthening our voices.

Our God-designed voice - our color - finds an expression that is deeper, richer, and fuller. The strengthening that happens as we go deeper allows us to express our colors in ways that impact and inspire others to express theirs.

In this final part of our journey, in the space between, we will strengthen our voices to be deeper, richer, and fuller expressions. We'll deepen our understanding of how to rest for what's ahead, of how to move forward for the next season, and of how to leave the right marks along the path for others.

SACRED INTERMISSIONS

"And the land had rest from war." // Joshua 14:15b

Pause.
Inhale deeply.
Exhale a long breath.

Caleb remained tenacious for 45 years believing for this moment. The moment when God's promises reached fulfillment. No more striving. No more waring. No more holding on to a promised future inheritance.

The land had rest from war.

Rest is God's invitation to embrace sacred intermissions.
When we rest, our awareness of our God-design increases.

Do you ever get caught up doing that you lose sight of your being? When we lose the sight of our being we lose sight of our purpose. This loss causes us to lose the tone of our voice. While the tension has a way of refining our voices in ways that can only happen in that space, the tension is also draining.

Cultivated Disciplines

In the first couple of months after I left my job as an attorney, I realized how drained I felt. When I was in the midst of it all, I hadn't fully realized that working two part-time jobs that required full-time hours from me had worn me down to the point of losing sight of my purpose. Because I jumped from project to project without sacred intermission of rest, I had lost the tone of my voice. I had been tenacious in the tension, but I needed rest from my striving. God invited me to embrace a sacred intermission.

I grew up performing in concerts where the first half was an hour-long four-movement symphony. I remember after playing the last note, we put our instruments down, the audience erupted in applause, and I exhaled the longest breath I had in me. Only to realize it was simply intermission. We had an entire second half of the concert to perform. We cleared the stage and went backstage for our 10-minute intermission before going back to finish the concert. Those 10 minutes were sacred to me. They gave me time to relax my hands, my arms, and my entire body from the hour of sustained playing. They gave me time to rest my mind from the race of reading notes on the sheet music and communicating what I read from my brain to my fingers to play. They gave me time to prepare for the second half of the concert.

During this sacred intermission time, I cultivated disciplines that allowed me to embrace those 10 minutes well. One of those disciplines was retuning my instrument. When I worked those strings hard for an hour or so, they would loosen and slip slightly out of tune. I needed to fine tune each string. The precision of fine tuning each string makes a huge difference to the overall intonation of the violin. This fine-tuning discipline trained my ears to increase my awareness of my experience, my instrument, and myself.

Increasing our awareness is the ultimate purpose of rest. Rest is not an invitation to space out; rest is an invitation to tune in. It's an invitation to tune into God's voice once again. God gives a promise of rest to those who have believed. To those who have tenaciously held on to God's voice there is an invitation to rest.

> "For we who have believed enter that rest, as he has said, "As I swore in my wrath, 'They shall not enter my rest...'" [Hebrews 4:3]

The writer of Hebrews connects the story of Moses and the Israelites who wandered in the wilderness with Joshua and the Israelites who inhabited the Promised Land. In verse 3, we see the author contrast between those who listened to God's voice and those who were disobedient to God's voice. Those who were obedient and believed entered into God's rest, while those who were not obedient never entered the rest of God. Caleb was one of the exceptional ones, like Joshua, who believed in the word of God, the voice of God, and the promises of God for his life. As a result of his faith, he had another promise: the promise of entering into God's rest.

In the sacred intermission of God's promised rest for those who believe, we cultivate disciplines that fine tune our voices, just like I did during intermission of my orchestra concerts. Our voices may not be dramatically out of tune, but like my violin, they may have gone slightly out of tune through the strain of striving for so long. We embrace God's invitation to a sacred intermission by reflecting on His words, recognizing His ways, and recommitting to His will.

Reflect on His word

After the Israelites entered into rest from years of striving, Joshua invited them to a covenant renewal ceremony at Shechem. The covenant renewal ceremony highlights two key features of the sacred intermission of rest. First, they come together for the purpose of renewal. Rest allows us to renew ourselves - to become new again. After the weariness of remaining tenacious in the tension, the Israelites needed renewal. The covenant renewal ceremony created space for the sacred purpose of renewal. This sacred purpose was complemented by being held at a sacred place. Shechem was the first place that Abraham went after the Lord spoke the promise that this land would be his land. It was the place where Abraham commits his life to that promise by setting up an altar. Shechem becomes a key place on the "Route of the Patriarchs," where Abraham, Isaac, and Jacob (the three patriarchs) traversed and experienced sacred intermissions there. It was the place Moses told Joshua and the Israelites to go once they entered the Promised Land to speak the words of the covenant.

We need revival. When we strive to tenaciously pursue and possess God's promises, we are depleting ourselves. We need to experience the renewal that comes through rest. God invites us into this sacred intermission for this sacred purpose. In this space, God gives us an opportunity to be made new again, to be transformed again, to be revived again into His image and likeness. And just as the Israelites experienced that sacred purpose in a sacred place, we need sacred places. Where are the sacred places you go to? Is there a sacred place where God declared His promise to you that you can return to? Perhaps you can't return to that place, because it's another state or country, but is there a way that you can bring the significance of that place to mind when you enter into a sacred intermission? The purpose and place of sacred intermissions of rest allow us to practice certain disciplines where we can increase our awareness of ourselves and God. One of those disciplines is reflecting on God's words, voice, and promises to us.

It's from this purpose and place that Joshua shares a historical account reflecting on the fulfillment of God's promises dating back to Abraham. He makes the connection between the current reality of the Israelites and the larger story they were part of in history. He closes his reflection with this God-spoken reminder:

> "I gave you a land on which you had not labored
> and cities that you had not built, and you dwell
> in them. You eat the fruit of vineyards and olive
> orchards that you did not plant." [Joshua 24:13]

These words were reminiscent of the words Moses spoke to these same Israelites before they entered into the Promised Land.

> "For the Lord your God is bringing you into a
> good land, a land of brooks of water, of fountains
> and springs, flowing out in the valleys and hills, a
> land of wheat and barley, of vines and fig trees and
> pomegranates, a land of olive trees and honey, a
> land in which you will eat bread without scarcity,
> in which you will lack nothing, a land whose
> stones are iron, and out of whose hills you can
> dig copper. And you shall eat and be full and you
> shall bless the Lord your God for the good land
> he has given you." [Deuteronomy 8:7-10]

On the other side of the promise, they can rest knowing God faithfully brought them into the land. And in this rest, they can respond by blessing the Lord for the good land he has given them.

I can't help but wonder, while Joshua is leading them in this general reflection of God's promises, if God's specific words of promise to Caleb were replaying through his mind. Maybe this has happened to you before: You're listening to the general application of a sermon and you're replaying the specific application of God to your life.

> "But my servant Caleb, because he has a different spirit and has followed me fully, I will bring in to the land into which he went and his descendant shall possess it." [Numbers 14:22-24]

Reflecting on the consistency of God's voice about His promises to His people must have been such an encouraging moment for the Israelites and for Caleb. On the other side of God's promises it's important to reflect on His words before and after the fulfillment. Sacred intermissions of rest allow us to recognize the consistency of God's voice. The weariness that comes from the tension often dulls the roar of God's voice to a whisper or even to silence. Sacred intermissions, renew our ears to hear God's voice again. As we read the word, as we listen to Him in prayer, and as we hear His words through others, reflecting on His voice reminds us that God's word is consistent and it never returns void. Reflecting on His words begins to fine tune our voice to respond rightly to His voice.

Before they entered the land, Moses told them in Deuteronomy that when they entered the land, they would bless the Lord for bringing them into the promise. In sacred intermissions, we respond rightly to God's voice with our gratitude. We bless the Lord by responding by thanking God that the fulfillment of His words and promises are His and His alone. As we embrace an awareness of what God has done, it creates a posture of gratitude in us towards God. Cultivating the discipline of reflection on

God's words creates the opportunity for response. As we practice responding with gratitude, we won't be able to stop overflowing with thanksgiving for all that God has fulfilled. As we utter thanksgivings, our voices are tuned to the goodness and kindness of God. Our reflection on God's voice is our opportunity to bless God with our voice. Reflection and response in the sacred intermission of rest refine our voice to its God-designed tone.

Recognize His ways

Through the reflection on God's words, Joshua then leads the people to recognize God's ways.

> "Now therefore fear the Lord and serve him in sincerity and in faithfulness. Put away the gods that your fathers served beyond the River and in Egypt, and serve the Lord." [Joshua 24:14]

Following God's ways means having a total faith in Him and not a partial faith in Him and in other gods. Following the ways of God requires an undivided faith that follows His path towards fulfillment of His promises to us. In this sacred intermission, Joshua moves from the word of God to the ways of God. In this way, he reminds them and us that we cannot only be hearers of the word. Also, we have to be doers of the word. Doers of the word recognize God's ways and seek to follow those ways. Doers of the word seek to turn towards God's ways and not away from His ways to follow other gods.

> "Then the people answered, "Far be it from us that we should forsake the Lord to serve other gods, for it is the Lord our God who brought us and our fathers up from the land of Egypt, out

of the house of slavery, and who did those great signs in our sight and preserved us in all the way that we went, and among all the people though whom we passed. And the Lord drove out before us all the peoples, the Amorites who lived in the land. Therefore we also will serve the Lord, for he is our God." [Joshua 24:16-18]

The Israelites respond to Joshua's invitation for them to recognize and follow God's ways with a resounding: "We DO recognize God's ways and we ARE following His ways." When we're holding on to God's promise in the tension, it's easy for our recognition of God's ways to become diluted. We look at others and assume that since God brought us into the fulfillment of His promises we must be following His ways. Maybe even without realizing it, we become overly confident and self-righteous. All the while, we are only partially recognizing and following His ways. But we couldn't see it. When we may become desensitized to just how different God's ways are compared to ours. Like the Israelites we proclaim with confidence: "We DO recognize God's ways and we ARE following His ways" when in fact we have unknowingly mixed God's ways with our ways.

"But Joshua said to the people, "You are not able to serve the Lord, for he is a holy God. He is a jealous God; he will not forgive your transgressions or your sins. If you forsake the Lord and serve foreign gods, then he will turn and do you harm and consume you after having done you good." And the people said to Joshua, "No, but we will serve the Lord." Then Joshua said to the people, "You are witnesses against yourselves that you have chosen the Lord, to serve him." And they said, "We are witnesses." He said,"Then put away

the foreign gods that are among you, and incline
your heart to the Lord, the God of Israel." [Joshua
24:19-22]

Joshua calls them out! He tells them they aren't able to fully serve
the Lord! They are following the ways of foreign gods. He leads
them to recognize that even though God brought them into the
good land and brought them into rest, if they don't recognize His
ways faithfully, then there will be consequences. He tells them
to "turn away from the foreign gods and incline their hearts to
the Lord." Joshua (and Caleb) have always spoken in faith and
through courage to lead the people into the promises of God, so
this confrontation shouldn't surprise us.

And it shouldn't surprise us that there is both a comforting
impact of God's word and a confronting impact. We will get
called out in our sacred intermissions. Cultivating the discipline
of recognition realigns us to God's ways. In this space of rest, we
learn to recognize how we've diluted His ways by mixing His
ways with our ways. We may not have "foreign gods" in the form
of statutes and images like the Israelites, but our "foreign gods"
are the earthly things we honor more than we honor God. Our
"foreign gods" come in the form of ideas, thoughts, people, or
tangible things that we allow to dictate our ways more than God's
ways dictate our ways. Even though God has been good to us, His
goodness is not an effect of our goodness. God's goodness is an
effect of His God-ness.

As we learn to recognize God's ways and our misalignments with
them, we learn to respond with confession. Confession is good;
confession is hard. Confession reveals our need and dependence
for God's ways over our own ways. When we speak words of
confession to God about how we've been unfaithful to Him and
insincere to Him, our voices find their true sound. Joshua helps

the Israelites recognize their need for confession by telling them to "put away the foreign gods that are among [them], and to incline [their] heart to the Lord, the God of Israel." The underlying theological concept here is repentance. Repentance is two-fold. The first part is reflected in Joshua's words when he says: "Put away." In Hebrew, this means to depart from or turn aside from. When we repent we turn away from something. Joshua goes on to say: "incline your heart to the Lord." The Hebrew word literally means to stretch out, extend, or bend. This is the second part of repentance. After we've turned away from something, we stretch out in a humble bending posture towards God. In particular, notice how Joshua says to "incline your hearts." This stretched out humble bending posture comes from our hearts. The posture starts at our core. In sacred intermissions, as we cultivate the discipline of recognition, we are provoked to respond with confession that starts with repentance.

> "Since therefore it remains for some to enter it, and those who formally received the good news failed to enter because of disobedience, again he appoints a certain day, "Today," saying through David so long afterward, in the words already quoted, "Today if you hear his voice, do not harden your hearts." [Hebrews 4:6-7]

The discipline of recognition that leads to confession allows us to enter His rest. We rest, when we recognize the sound of His voice that teaches us His ways. As we recognize His ways and confess our departure, our hearts are softened. Today, we can hear His words. Today, we can recognize His ways. Today, we can keep our hearts soft through confession. Today, we can embrace His sacred intermission by recognizing our misalignments from His ways. Today, we can depend on Him to return to the only ways that truly help us find our voice. This confession response fine tunes those slight departures from God's ways that we may not have realized. As we fine tune our ways through confession, our voices are fine tuned for the part of our story that comes after intermission.

Recommit to His will

In the sacred intermission of rest, God's voice calls us to recommit to His will. Our striving to hold on to the promises of God can lead our commitment to God's will to become routine. But when we enter into His promised rest, His words compel our recommitment.

Hear Joshua's words to the people during the covenant renewal ceremony:

> "And the people said to Joshua, "The Lord our God we will serve and his voice we will obey. So Joshua made a covenant with the people that day, and put in place statutes and rules for them at Shechem. And Joshua wrote these words in the Book of the Law of God. And he took a large stone and set it up there under the terebinth that was by the sanctuary of the Lord. And Joshua said to all the people, "Behold, this stone shall be a witness against us, for it has heard all the words of the Lord that he spoke to us. Therefore it shall be a witness against you, lest you deal falsely with your God." So Joshua sent the people away, every man to his inheritance." [Joshua 24:24]

This recommitment comes on the heels of the people's confession of their departure from God's ways. The people's two-part response teaches us about the nature of commitment and recommitment. In the first part of their response, they say "we will serve." They use the Hebrew word for "work" or "enslavement" to describe the relationship of their commitment to God. When we commit to something, we align ourselves in surrender to that thing, while simultaneously rejecting our alignment with other things. So, in the first part of the people's recommitment they conjure up the images of alignment in surrender to another. As workers, we surrender to an employer. As slaves, we surrender to a master. With this response by the people, we see that commitment should not be taken lightly.

Think about it this way: Your commitment to soup instead of salad, basically means that you've rejected the salad. We struggle with commitment in our culture. Commitment challenges us to stand firm for something at the cost of losing something else. The cost of commitment to God is great and it can be challenging when we don't enter a space where we can consider the cost. In the space of rest, we understand the significance of commitment. In the emptiness of rest, we sense the fullness of commitment.

In the second part of the people's response, they say: "we will obey." "Obey" here is the word "shama." When the Israelites say "shama", they make a commitment to hear and understand God's voice. This is obedience. The root word for obey here is "shama." As the second part of their commitment, the people respond by saying they will hear and understand God's voice. Committing to serve God is empty without an equal commitment to hear and understand His voice. This response to hear and understand God's voice is a commitment to be perceptive and discerning when God is speaking. There is a quieting that happens in sacred intermissions. The chaos of our striving stops. The ongoing hum of what we need to do ceases and the clarity of who we're called to commit to resounds. When we begin to perceive God and his will with this kind of clarity, then our work for Him has significance. Rest helps to discern that committing to God's will is not simply doing things for God, but it's becoming more like Him and reflecting Him to a world that needs Him. In the quiet of rest, we hear the call of commitment. We hear God's will for us: "As you align in surrender to your God-design and your God-designed voice, you will speak my truth."

> "So Joshua made a covenant with the people that day, and put in place statutes and rules for them at Shechem. And Joshua wrote these words in the Book of the Law of God. And he took a large stone and set it up there under the terebinth that was by the sanctuary of the Lord. And Joshua said to all the people, "Behold, this stone shall be a witness against us, for it has heard all the words of the Lord that he spoke to us. Therefore it shall be a witness against you, lest you deal falsely with your God." So Joshua sent the people away, every man to his inheritance." [Joshua 24:25-28]

The purpose of this sacred intermission was ultimately for the people to renew their covenant with the Lord. In this sacred moment, the people could respond to what the Lord wanted to do with and through His people. As you were reading, did you notice the stone Joshua set up as a witness of their commitment? We've seen stones before, when the Israelites beheld the wonder in the tension as the Lord brought them through the Jordan River. At that time, Joshua set up stones as a reminder of the inexplicably awe-inspiring act of God on the people's behalf. Here, Joshua uses the stones as a reminder of their recommitment to God's will. Stones mark the moments. This was a moment of internal commitment marked with a visual representation. As we enter into the sacred intermission of rest, we have a beautiful opportunity to mark the moments - to find visual representations of our internal commitments to God's will. Those visual representations anchor us as we continue to strive towards the fulfillment of God's promises.

The covenant renewal ceremony ends with Joshua sending the people to inhabit their inheritance. As we accept the invitation to embrace the sacred intermissions of rest, we will find ourselves empowered to possess God's promises with new vitality.

In sacred intermissions, our reflection on God's word provokes our response of gratitude for all that God has done and given. Our recognition of God's ways invites our response of confession about how our ways have departed from His ways. Our recommitment to God's will ushers our response of service and obedience.

This is the beauty of sacred intermissions. In rest, we strengthen our voices to continue possessing our inheritance.

Color You _____ Moment

Color Exercise: Play the Pauses

One of my conductors always used to tell us that when there were rests in the music (spaces where we didn't play, but other instruments continued to play), we needed to "play the pauses." Essentially, he was telling us not to zone out just because we weren't playing, but to stay connected to the music. Play the pauses.

This wisdom can enhance our understanding of rest - the sacred intermission. Sometime this week, I want to invite you to play the pauses. It doesn't need to be an entire day or even a lot of hours in a day. But I want to invite you to pause, to rest, to enjoy a sacred intermission.

How to Play the Pauses:

- Determine your purpose for seeking renewal this week
    - *For example, I want to seek renewal for my mind that has been overloaded by a long to do list. Or, I want to seek renewal for my soul that has felt lifeless and drained.*
- Designate a place where you can fulfill that purpose
    - *For example, at a place that holds significance for you, at a coffee shop, at a lake, etc.*
- Engage with God's Word in a way that can fulfill your purpose for seeking renewal
    - *For example, reading a particular Psalm you love, listening to a sermon podcast, etc.*
- Reflect on how God's Word is both comforting you and confronting you
    - *For example, you could jot notes in a journal, write a poem, draw a picture, etc.*
- Confess your needs to God and your departures from His ways
    - *For example, you could have a conversation with God and/or continue to write notes in a journal, write a poem, draw a picture, etc.*
- Commit to serve and obey God in some specific way according to what your conversation with each other has revealed about your purpose for seeking renewal
    - *For example, I will create a "to not do list" alongside my to do list that keeps me balanced. Or, I will intentionally reach out to a life-giving friend to speak life into my lifeless and drained soul.*

ANOTHER DAY LATER ON

"I ain't done, I ain't done,
As long as there's breath in my lungs,
I ain't done" // Andy Mineo, I: The Arrow

When we stop transforming, we start dying. Caleb's story did not end at Hebron. The inheritance of Hebron was only a partial fulfillment of the Lord's promise. There was more for Caleb. He was part of a community who was part of a larger narrative. Yes, there was rest for the land. But that rest was simply a sacred intermission. There was more land for Caleb's community of Israelites to conquer before they possessed the promise. And even when that Promised Land was possessed, there was still more. There is a Promised Land we will possess for all eternity. As long as we are on this side of eternity, we are in the tension. God graciously allows us to experience partial fulfillments of His promises. These partial fulfillments guide us to find our voice, but the journey is not over.

After the rest, the journey of transformation in the tension continues. When we realize our transformation isn't over, we find a new freedom to use our voices as they continue to conform to God's voice. We discover that the God-designed voice within calls into existence the things that do not exist.[62] Our awareness of the partial fulfillment of God's promises on this side of eternity unveils to us how God's voice is tethered to immeasurably more than we can think or imagine. This truth gives us the freedom to realize that our God-designed voices are also tethered to something more. The limits of our temporal experience, don't mean we speak with limitations. We speak with an openness to the possibilities. We lean forward. We press on.

Climb the Next Mountain

In the previous chapter, we looked at the promise of rest in the letter written to the Hebrews. Using the story of the Israelites in the desert and the Promised Land, the writer speaks of rest as a promise for those who have faith and those who hear God's voice. There's another part of that promise.

> "For if Joshua had given them rest, God would not have spoken of another day later on. So then, there remains a Sabbath rest for the people of God, for whoever has entered God's rest has also rested from his works as God did from his work.
>
> Let us therefore, strive to enter that rest, so that no one may fall by the same sort of disobedience."
> [Hebrews 4:8-11]

The writer talks about "another day later on." Here, we are taught that there remains a rest for us. We are encouraged to "strive to enter that rest." While the partial fulfillment of God's promises reveal the limits of our experiences on this side of eternity, they also teach us to strive for eternal rest. The partial fulfillment compels us to strive for "another day later on" when we will experience the complete fulfillment of the promises of God. The writer of Hebrews challenges us to strive. This striving is not us trying to making things happen on our own. Here, to strive is challenging us to act fervently to obtain all that God has assigned to us through faith. A seemingly paradoxical reality exists where even as we find stillness in rest, we still move towards the rest that God has for us. We find rest, while striving for a greater rest. We experience the sacredness of intermissions and we yearn to climb the next mountain. A mountain that brings us closer to "another day later on."

Alfred Lord Tennyson said it best in his poem "Ulysses." He writes of a mythical hero who returns home after countless travels and finds himself restless to explore again.

> We are not now that strength which in old days
> Moved earth and heaven, that which we are,
> we are;
> One equal temper of heroic hearts,
> Made weak by time and fate, but strong in will
> To strive, to seek, to find, and not to yield.

I can imagine Caleb saying these words. At an old age, the hero leader of the tribe of Judah, restless to explore again strives for "another day later on." Caleb's motivation was just as strong as it had been the day he reported the land that he saw that was exceedingly good. Although he experienced rest, he strived for more. After Caleb drives out the sons of Anak, those giants possessing the promise, Caleb climbs the next mountain.

> "And he [Caleb] went up from there against the inhabitants of Debir." [Joshua 15:15]

The geographical insights of this verse are that Caleb climbed another mountain range. Caleb is the poster child for Tennyson's "to strive, to seek, to find, and not to yield." After going to war to possess the mountain range in Hebron, Caleb - knowing the limits, but not living with limitations - climbs another mountain. Oh, that it would be said of us that even when we have conquered one mountain, we never stopped climbing mountains. If someone wrote a biography about my life I would want the title to be: She Never Stopped Climbing Mountains. I want to live so tethered to eternity that I'm pulled to climb the next mountain until Christ calls me to my forever home. I want to tell the stories of who I became with each mountain I climbed. I want my family and friends to say about me: "she never stopped climbing mountains". With every mountain we climb we are transformed more into the fullness of our God-design.

I'm not sure where you find yourself in the tension between God's promises and their fulfillment. But I am certain that when you've possessed one mountain and rested from that possession, there are more mountains to climb. Every mountain you climb invites you into a newly unfolding part of your story where you will face challenging and exciting new experiences. With every mountain you climb, on this side of eternity, you experience new dimensions of God. These dimensions of God give you the opportunity to experience new dimensions of your voice. As you climb the next mountain, your voice is transformed more and more into an echo of Heaven. With every mountain climbed, your voice draws heaven near for you and for the communities God has entrusted to you. Climb the next mountain.

Run With Endurance

As we lean forward and press on in the tension, there will be moments of weariness. In the aftermath of possessing a promise and resting from that promise, complacency may settle upon us. When adrenaline wears out, the momentum that catapulted us into possession of the promise is gone.

The writer of Hebrews speaks to a community of Hebrew Christians waiting desperately for the coming Messiah. They were persecuted and became weary waiting for "another day later on." They lost the momentum that once drove their faith. Have you ever been there?

Against this backdrop, the writer of Hebrews tells the stories of the heroes of the faith. These men and women part of their history (and ours), who continued on in the tension, though they would not see the complete fulfillment of God's promises on this side of heaven. Yet, they believed for "another day later on." After the writer tells their stories, we hear this encouragement:

> "Therefore, since we are surrounded by so great a cloud of witnesses [the heroic men and women], let us also lay aside every weight, and sin which clings so closely, and let us run with endurance the race that is set before us, looking to Jesus, the founder and perfecter of our faith, who for the joy that was set before him endured the cross, despising the shame, and is seated at the right hand of the throne of God." [Hebrews 12:1-2]

We all need encouragement. I don't care how strong you are or how capable you are. We all need encouragement. Even on our best days we can grow weary. The Hebrews receive their encouragement from a great cloud of witnesses. I like to think of this as a great cloud of cheerleaders. They're cheering for your colors: "Go yellow! Go blue! Go red! Go green!" With the encouragement of our cheerleaders, we are empowered to throw off the weight of complacency, untangle from the sin of disobedience, and run with endurance. To "run with endurance" means to progress with full effort towards a directed purpose in a steadfast manner. Just because there is a limit to the complete fulfillment of His promises on this side of eternity, does not mean there is not a purpose in our pursuit. As we pursue the promises of God, we discover that progressing towards them produces discipline in us that allows us to share in His holiness.

> "It is for discipline that you have to endure…he disciplines us for our good, that we may share his holiness. For the moment all discipline seems painful rather than pleasant, but later it yields the peaceful fruit of righteousness to those who have been trained by it." [Hebrews 12:7a, 10b-11]

As we pursue the race set before us with a steadfastness pursuit, our voices are trained. Sometimes the training will be painful. We'll say things that get us in trouble. We'll be quick to speak and slow to listen. We'll be corrected and even rebuked by the Holy Spirit - sometimes directly and sometimes by our brothers and sisters in Christ. But you can be certain of this, the disciplining of our voices as we run with endurance produces the fruit of righteousness in our lives. When we speak, the fruit of our speech will taste sweet to those who hear us.

> "Therefore, lift your drooping hands and strengthen your weak knees, and make straight paths for your feet, so that what is lame may not

be put out of joint but rather be healed." [Hebrews 12:12-13]

Running with endurance means a surrender to discipline. The kind of discipline that invites us to action. To get up and restore hands and knees that have atrophied. To be proactive towards an aim and purpose. In that proactive discipline, we find healing to everything that has become weak, weary, and exhausted.

I'll be honest. I wish healing could come from hiding under a blanket and letting the season of weariness pass. If I ignore it, it will just go away. But that doesn't actually work. Running with endurance when all we want to do is hide is hard work.

After dad left us for his heavenly home, we were left with this enormous hole that his presence once filled. Even now when I go home to our home in Florida, I can feel his presence pouring out of the walls. His words, prayers, and even his silence is so permeated in the walls that his shadow brightly hovers over us. But the hole was there. My approach to this emptiness was to hide under my green blankie and hope for the season to pass, justifying it by thinking: we all deal with grief in different ways, right? But my brother had a completely different approach. One, that in retrospect, I admire. He ran. He literally ran.

Let me give you context that my brother is not someone people - himself included - would consider a runner. He was the kid who had such bad asthma growing up that he used a nebulizer. I'm also pretty sure that when our papa passed away he was at the heaviest weight of his life. Yet, he ran. I have no idea how, but he did. He cultivated the discipline of getting up early, before the sun in hot and humid central Florida and before his two very little girls, to simply run.

Now, while I admire that act of running on its own, what struck me most about him running was his intention.

> "So I do not run aimlessly; I do not box as one beating the air. But I discipline my body and keep it under control lest after preaching to others I myself should be disqualified." [1 Corinthians 9:26-27]

This verse was his intention. On the 2nd anniversary of our papa's heavenly birthday, he wrote about it on Instagram this way:

> "2 years ago, I made a decision to change how I treated my body. I didn't really do it for me. I did it for my father; for my family. I told myself if I was strong enough, I could carry them; I could be their strength. However, the more I put my body through this process, the more I learned how to let go. I learned how to trust not in myself, but in God. It's become a discipline that I have incorporated into every part of my life. #running #runharder #runfaster #runforpapa"

My brother had an aim. He had a purpose in his pursuit. He did not run aimlessly. There was certainty in the intention behind why he was running. An intention that he could clearly see even though it's not something that's clearly seen. By his own admission, running with endurance became a discipline. I can attest that it has changed his life. The discipline of running with endurance did a work of healing in him that has produced the fruit of righteousness. He's become more Christ-like, more Kingdom-minded, and more attuned with his God-designed voice. He uses his voice now in a way that I've never heard him use it. He uses it to speak for the greater things ahead. His voice is becoming an echo of Heaven on earth. Run with endurance.

Live On the Edge

Rend Collective said it best in their Campfire Stories devotional:

> "God loves us too deeply to smother us with
> safety. He knows we don't combat our fears by
> living sheltered lives - we fight fear by developing
> courage. And courage is forged in the dangerous
> furnace flame of risk. The "life in all its fullness"
> that Jesus talks about in John, is not a pain-free
> life or a failure-proof life, but a passionate life. We
> need to stop thinking of the gospel as an insurance
> policy against getting hurt and rather as a license
> to dream big and risk big for the Kingdom, in the
> assurance that if it all "goes wrong", grace will
> pick us up, dust us off and throw us right back
> into the action."

As we climb the next mountain and run with endurance, we find
that in the continued tension we can live on the edge. If we are
going to continue in the process of transformation, then why not
live on the edge of it? Why not accept "the gospel as a license to
dream big and risk big for the Kingdom"? Why not let the furnace
flame forge a courageous voice?

My grandparents live in Puerto Rico on the northwestern part
of the island in a mountain-town called San Sebastian. I hadn't
been to Puerto Rico in ten years, so in 2016 when I visited the
island, I wanted to explore the areas around San Sebastian.
We went to caves, waterfalls, a coffee factory, and several other
beautiful places, but my favorite place was Las Ruinas (the ruins,
in English). Las Ruinas was the Borinquen Point Lighthouse built
in 1889 by the Spaniards. The Spaniards used elaborate brick
architecture to construct the lighthouse, so when it was originally

built, the lighthouse was a beautiful marvel on the coastline. But in 1918, there was a devastating earthquake off the northwestern coast of Puerto Rico that damaged the lighthouse beyond repair. That's when it became Las Ruinas. (Travel Tip: The Borinquen Point Lighthouse was rebuilt by the US Coast Guard a little further down the coast, so if you're looking for Las Ruinas make sure that you Google the original location)

To get to Las Ruinas, you drive through a golf course and down a dirt road. My mom was in the car with me and I'm pretty sure she thought I was losing it chasing this wonder. It was the best of off-the-beaten-path adventuring! As we drove further down this dirt road, we didn't see the lighthouse. We were curious if we were going to see a lighthouse at all. But then it came into view as we drove closer towards the coast. What you see when you come upon the ruins are two brick walls with some damage and then the side of the lighthouse that faces the ocean is in complete disarray. It was beautiful. Here we stood, 127 years after the lighthouse was built on the coastline of the island, in the ruins. Off-the-beaten-path, we heard the sound of the waves crashing up against the rocks on the shoreline below the lighthouse.

We loved it so much, the next day, we brought my grandparents, my aunts, and my cousin to see this withered marvel. This time, those crashing waves called my name. I wanted to stand on the edge. I wanted to hear the voice of the waves crashing up against the rocks and imagine what this beautiful lighthouse was like when it was built. I wanted to feel what the broken down brick walls must have felt like with the wave and winds hitting them in the midst of a storm. So, I traversed the boulders and made my way to the edge.

There's something enlivening about going deeper and further than you have before. When you set out to live on the edge of what seems possible, what seemed ruined in your life starts to come alive. When you set out towards the edge, it's almost unimaginable to ever go back. On the edge, the wind is stronger, the waves are louder, and the experience is so personal that everything in you and around you comes alive. When you start to live life on the edge, you get a front row seat to God's wonder-working power.

I nearly gave my abuelo a heart attack as I jumped from rock to rock to make it to the edge. When you start to live life on the edge of what seems possible, the people watching you are probably going to think you've lost it and when they love you you'll probably almost give them a heart attack too. But standing on the edge, I looked out at the ocean and I beheld God's majesty. I could hear the voice of God in the waves and winds. His voice sounded like a timpani - deep, resonant, and strong. A voice that boomed inside the cavity of my soul and filled me up so completely that everything else was drowned out. It was as though those crashing waves were filling everything inside of me and bringing me to life.

There are countless stories I could tell you about moments when I have set out towards the edge. On the edge of Grand Canyon, on the edge of a mountain, or on the edge of a crazy idea. Living on the edge has taught me what it means that I've been "born again to a living hope through the resurrection of Jesus Christ from the dead."[63] Peter - one of Jesus's closest friends and disciples - knew how to live life on the edge. This is the guy who walked on water. This is the guy who jumped out of the boat after Jesus's resurrection. This is the guy who preached a life-altering sermon and 3,000 people received and believed Jesus was the Messiah. Peter lived on the edge. So, when he writes in a letter to an exiled and persecuted community living life in the ruins, his encouragement about being born again to a living hope is powerfully authentic.

"Blessed be the God and father of our Lord Jesus Christ! According to his great mercy, he has caused us to be born again to a living hope through the resurrection of Jesus Christ from the dead, to an inheritance that is imperishable, undefiled, and unfading, kept in heaven for you, who by God's power are being guarded through faith for a salvation ready to be revealed in the last time." [1 Peter 1:3-5]

These verses fill me - like those crashing waves - with living hope to live on the edge! Here's the deep truth Peter is conveying: God's loyalty compels His mercy towards us and revives us to new life by hope to hope for a future that is secured in the present and guarded by His power. (There's a lot packed in to that sentence, so read it one more time.) A living hope is God's gift of alive expectation of a future promise that is certain in the present. The imperishable, undefiled, and unfading inheritance God guards for us is the Heavenly Promised Land. It's not the earthly, limited promises that are partially fulfilled. It's the heavenly, limitless promises that are fully fulfilled. The living hope is where we find the security to live life on the edge. We can live a life that is wholly expectant that the fullness of God's future promises are presently reserved for us by God's power.

I love what Paul writes about Abraham: "In hope he believed against hope, that he should become the father of many nations, as he had been told, 'So shall your offspring be.'"[64] In hope, he believed against hope. Abraham put all his weight on the promises of God and hoped against hope. He had no reason to believe that in Sarah's and his old age life would come out of barrenness. But Abraham lived on the edge of the promises of God with a living hope that caused the ruins of barrenness in Sarah and his life to give birth to new life.

When hope is revived in our hearts, we like Abraham, can hope against hope. We can be free to dream big and risk big, because the gospel frees us to life, an abundant life. A life where we set out to live on the edge of what God has for us. A life where the ruins are revived. The impossible becomes possible. My brother wrote a song that says: "Where the sidewalk ends my life begins." Living at the edge of the limit this side of eternity, brings us into the limitlessness of God. As we live on the edge with an alive expectation of a future that is presently certain, God's timpani voice reverberates in the abyss of our soul and everything in us comes alive.

The gospel gives you permission to live on the edge. When we think there was nothing but ruins, living on the edge transforms us. What we experience on the edge changes the way we see. When your perspective transforms, your language transforms. You can't speak the same way again after the ruins have been born again. Live on the edge.

"Burn Out Bright"

"If we've only got one try, if we've only got one life, if time was never on our side, before I die I wanna burn out bright." Switchfoot, one of my favorite bands of all-time, wrote these words and so many other words that carried and continue to carry me through seasons of my life. Climbing the next mountain, running with endurance, and living on the edge all point to the chorus of this Switchfoot song, "Burn Out Bright." On this side of eternity, we remain in the tension, and we can choose to allow God to transform our lives and our voices in incredible ways that empower us to burn out bright.

"Since we have such a hope, we are very bold, not like Moses, who would put a veil over his face so that the Israelites might not gaze at the outcome of what was being brought to an end. But their minds were hardened. For to this day, when they read the old covenant, that same veil remains unlifted, because only through Christ is it taken away. Yet to this day whenever Moses is read a veil lies over their hearts. But when one turns to the Lord, the veil is removed. Now the Lord is the Spirit, and where the Spirit of the Lord is, there is freedom. And we all with unveiled face, beholding the glory of the Lord, are being transformed into the same image from one degree of glory to another. For this comes from Lord who is the Spirit." [2 Corinthians 3:12-18]

A little Old Testament history about Moses and the Israelites reminds us that on Mount Sinai Moses told the Lord: "Please, show me your glory."[65] The Lord didn't show Moses His face, but instead put Moses in the nook of a rock and God's glory passed over him. When Moses came down from Mount Sinai, his nuclear radiant face caused the Israelites to place a veil over him. As we fast forward to the words from Paul in 2 Corinthians, he picks up on this story pointing to our living hope, saying that "we are very bold, not like Moses." Paul tells us that when we turn to the Lord "the veil is removed." The removal of the veil allows us to behold the glory of the Lord in a greater way than the Old Testament experience. We see a greater glory. A glory that transforms us into the image of Christ "from one degree of glory to another."

Doxa, the Greek word Paul uses for glory, means God's infinite, intrinsic worth. Doxa relates to the Hebrew word kobo meaning to be heavy. As we turn to God in the tension, we behold Him as though looking in a mirror and we transform into His image from one degree of infinitely heavy worth to the next degree of infinitely heavy worth. We burn with His glory - not a light that fades, but a burning substance that weighs into eternity. I want to burn out bright. I want the weight of my worth in the tension to burn brighter and brighter as the glory of God on Earth as in Heaven.

Our hope allows us to behold God's glory and transform from one degree of infinitely heavy worth to the next, and it's our faith that sustains the weight of our worth. As we behold God's glory, we burn bright with glory. Burning out bright invites us to a life of radical faith that sends light beams into the future.

The Message transliteration of the Bible gives us an inspiring articulation of the impact of burning out bright and sending light beams into the future:

"By an act of faith, Isaac reached into the future and he blessed Jacob and Esau." [Hebrews 11:20]

What a beautiful way to live a life that burns out bright. Isaac's faith sustained the glorious man of God he was becoming, because of the promises he received from God about him and his sons. His faith gave him vision to see the future. Isaac wasn't passive about what he saw; he acted on the unseen future and promises. He reached into the future and spoke blessings on his sons. This is what the faith of someone who burns out bright does. They have the light rays of faith that burn so bright that they can reach into the future and speak promises and inheritance into the next generation.

This verse is one of the reason I'm committed to investing in young people. When I first started working with middle school students twelve years ago, I asked God to give me a faith that saw each young person as He sees them. "Give me your vision about your children, so that I can see them through the eyes of faith." This prayer has been released from my mouth, my heart, my soul, and my mind countless times. I cannot tell you how many ways God has honored that prayer. That prayer has formed a bright faith in me like Isaac had towards his sons. Now, it's a prayer that I not only pray for young people, but also a prayer for everyone I come into contact with, so that I see others through the eyes of faith with beams of light.

Even though there are limits to the fullness of God's promises on this side of eternity, we can burn out bright. The light that we invite Christ to sustain in us through our hope and faith sends bright beams into the future impacting the lives of those around us. We can burn as spiritual fireballs building God's Kingdom in the spaces that need the spark of His presence.

Jack Kerouac said it well in his book, <u>On The Road</u>:

> "the only people for me are the mad ones, the ones who are mad to live, mad to talk, mad to be saved, desirous of everything at the same time, the ones who never yawn or say a commonplace thing, but burn, burn, burn like fabulous yellow roman candles exploding like spiders across the stars and in the middle you see the blue centerlight pop and everybody goes "Awww!"

I want to be one of the mad ones, that burn, burn, burn with the brightness of God's holy light and inspires others to burn out bright.

The tension isn't over. There is a limit to the fullness we can experience on this side of eternity. Let us not allow this reality, to cause us to conform to the path of least resistance or to let our vocal muscles atrophy from lack of development. Let's use this reality to compel us to strive towards a future that our spirits see. We aren't chasing shadows and we aren't striving after the wind. We are leaning towards the Heavenly Promised Land that is tethered to our souls.

> "So we do not lose heart. Though our outer self is wasting away, our inner self is being renewed day by day. For this light momentary affliction is preparing for us an eternal weight of glory beyond all comparison, as we look not to the things that are seen but to the things that are unseen. For the things that are seen are transient, but the things that are unseen are eternal." [2 Corinthians 4:16-18]

Let's live day-by-day seeking to live as close to that limit as possible. In the tension, we can choose to allow God to transform our voices into an echo of Heaven. On this side of eternity, our transformation is not over. God continues shaping us and molding us as our souls look towards "another day later on." There are still mountains to climb, there's a race to be run, there's an edge to reach, and there's a light that can burn, burn, burn out bright.

Color You _____ Moment

Questions to Ponder:
• How can the realization that on this side of eternity we only experience a partial fulfillment of God's promises encourage you to strengthen your voice?

- What are some of the possibilities in the season ahead for you on your journey between God's promises and their fulfillment?
- Based on the voice you've uncovered and refined throughout your journey, how can you speak into those possibilities?

Coloring Exercise: Color You Mantras

The four sections of this chapter reflect my core mantras:
1. Climb the next mountain
2. Run with endurance
3. Live on the edge
4. Burn out bright

In Sanskrit, "mantra" means a thought behind speech or action. Our Hindu and Buddhist brothers and sister use mantras as words or sounds repeated in meditation. We learn from their ancient practice about the significance of core thoughts that impact our speech. Mantras can strengthen our voices. These four Color Me Yellow Mantras have strengthened my voice and now it's your turn to develop your own Color You _____ Mantras.

- Make a list of as many words/phrase that resurface frequently, lines from poems, lyrics from songs, graffiti on walls, verses in the Bible, etc. that have impacted you.
- Why have these words, phrases, and/or lines impacted you?
- From this list, underline or circle core thoughts that can impact your voice
- Based on the list, write 3-5 words or phrases as your own Color You _____ Mantras (they could be rewrites from the list, combination of lines from the list, or your own remixes of the word or phrase from the list)

WHAT DO YOU WANT?

"The colors we use to paint our own lives splash all over the souls of those who are close to us." // Erwin Raphael McManus, The Artisan Soul

The color we add to the canvas of God's creation leaves an indelible mark. Our color leaves a mark of inspiration that activates other colors and continues God's masterpiece. Your voice carries a legacy. Finding your voice in the tension between God's promises and their fulfillment is not about you. It's about what God wants to do to you through you for others. The color you uncover within yourself is ultimately a reflection of God's legacy - the movement of His story that began in the beginning. In your voice, heaven and earth collide. In your voice, the Kingdom of God is at hand. In your voice, there's a catalyst that sparks potential in others.

"Death and life are in the power of the tongue."[66] Our voices - these vibrant colors inside us - carry a power that when released can build others up or break others down. In the book of James, he compares the tongue to a fire, saying that a small fire can set an entire forest ablaze. James reminds us to be quick to listen and slow to speak. We carry something powerful in our mouths. A tongue that allows us to speak and leaves marks on the people around us. Language impacts culture. Language impacts change.

Language leaves marks. Language leaves a legacy. As we realize the power we carry, we must ask ourselves: is my voice - my God-designed color - simply leaving a mark or is my voice leaving the right mark?

The right mark is an indelible mark of inspiration that activates other colors and continues God's masterpiece.

Last Words

Our journey with Caleb has revealed that even though his words were few, his marks were indelible. After Caleb and the people of Judah went up to Debir, Caleb announces that "whoever strikes Kiriath-sepher (Debir) and captures it, to him will I [Caleb] give Achsah my daughter as wife."[67] Othniel, Caleb's nephew, captured Debir and as promised received Achsah as his wife. There's a new marriage in the family, and Othniel and Achsah received a significant amount of property in the southern part of the Promised Land.

But the story doesn't end there. Afterward, we read a powerful exchange between a father and daughter.

> "...And she got off her donkey, and Caleb said to her, 'What do you want?' She said to him, 'Give me a blessing. Since you have given me the land of the Negeb, give me also springs of water.' And he gave her the upper springs and the lower springs."
> [Joshua 15:18b-19]

Let's zoom in on this conversation for a moment and make some observations about the context of this conversation. First, up until this point we've seen Caleb as a young leader exploring the

Promised Land, a tribal leader of Judah, and an elderly leader still fighting for the promises of God. Now, we hear from Caleb as father. We move away from seeing him on the frontline of a collective movement. Here, we see him at the frontline of his family. We hear the voice of Caleb in an intimate conversation between family - between a father and daughter.

Caleb had four children: three sons and one daughter.[68] His family traveled with him into the Promised Land. They saw him lead the tribe of Judah. They heard him speak about the promise of Hebron. They listened to his stories about Moses, about exploring the Promised Land, about the fearful young leaders with him, about his friendship with Joshua, and countless other stories that brought him and their family to this point. His values, mindset, and vision would have left an indelible mark on his family as they watched, listened, and lived this journey alongside him. As a family, they would have known the God-designed color that Caleb was leaving on the masterpiece of God's story. They would have been marked by the color. They would have been inspired by the right marks of Caleb's legacy.

Caleb's only daughter, Achsah - a girl among three boys. Her name means both "adorned" and "bursting the veil." As the only daughter, she was likely adorned by her father. He likely loved her as the apple of his eye and his pride and joy. We can imagine from the way that she approaches her father that she was like him: courageous. She comes courageously before her dad, bursting through the veil of "traditional" roles of females in this ancient culture, to make a request. In their conversation, while Achsah makes the first physical move by getting off the donkey to approach her father, Caleb speaks first: "What do you want?"

With these four words spoken by Caleb, he activated what was inside Achsah. He activated her voice. As you breathe out the inspiration of your color, it can be the activation of someone else's color. When you use the borrowed breath in your lungs to release inspiration into others, something powerful happens to and for others through you. In four simple words, Caleb called Achsah's voice out of her. Questions are a powerful mode of activation. Questions carry within them an underlying direction. Every question we ask is pointing the one we ask the question of in a particular direction. The power in this question pointed Achsah towards the courageous conviction. The same courageous conviction her father had that led him to make audacious asks. Caleb knew what he was promised and therefore he knew what he wanted. So, his color had contained courageous conviction and by asking his daughter, "What do you want?", he activated courageous conviction in her.

This was one of Jesus's favorite questions to ask during his earthly ministry. So many healings are activated through this question. It's a powerful question, because it invites people to make faith declarations with their voices. It's an inspiring question, because it draws on our deepest desires and visions. It's a question that causes what we believe to burst through our mouths. As our beliefs burst through, we begin to speak life into what we believe. "What do you want?" sets the vision in motion. When Caleb asks his daughter this question, his inspiration sets in motion the activation of the vision God had given her. The color in her was now the color that was bursting out of her. In a tangible way, Achsah was "bursting the veil" and stepping into her legacy.

What do you want?

There's a scene from the movie, *The Notebook*, where Noah asks Allie: What do you want? (If you've never seen this classic piece of film, you need to either go youtube the scene (type "what do you want the notebook" into the search bar) or stop reading now and watch the whole movie!)

For context: Noah and Allie were teenage sweethearts who "shouldn't have been together." They were from different socio-economic classes and Allie's parents didn't want them together. They have one of those iconic movie-scripted summers together filled with romance and fun. Then, Allie's parents force her to move away for school to get her away from Noah. He writes her letters every day that Allie's mom intercepts, so that the letters never get to Allie. And just like that, the romance is over. Fast forward: (I won't give too many details, because you really should watch the movie!) Allie and Noah reconnect, but Allie is engaged. The feelings between the two are messy and complicated. And then the iconic moment happens:

> Noah: So it's not gonna be easy. It's gonna be really hard. And we're gonna have to work at this every day. But I want to do that, because I want you. I want all of you, forever, you and me, every day. Can you do something for me? Please? Will you just picture your life for me? Thirty years from now? Forty years from now? What's it look like? If it's with that guy, go. Go! I lost you once. I think I can do it again, if I thought that's what you really wanted. But don't you take the easy way out.

> Allie: What easy way? There is no easy way. No matter what I do, somebody gets hurt!

> Noah: Would you stop thinking about what everyone wants?! Stop thinking about what I want, what he wants, what your parents want. What do you want? What do you want?

Allie: It's not that simple!

Noah: What do you want? What do you want?

Allie: I have to go.

I can't help but read Caleb's question to Achsah and hear Noah's question to Allie. Maybe I've watched The Notebook way too many times. But Noah is so emphatic with Allie. I love it. He wants to draw her voice out of her. Her true desires. Her true vision for her life. So, again and again he asks her: "What do you want?" He's emphatic with this question. I imagine that Caleb - even though he asked once - was equally emphatic. I imagine that when the Lord asks us what we want, He too is equally emphatic. And then I think we - like Allie - are equally unclear. More often than not, we answer God's question saying: "It's not that simple! I have to go." We've connected to the Lord by grace through faith. We've been awakened to our true desires, our true design, and our true promises. But we are too scared to activate our voice. We're too scared to speak with courageous conviction, because that means taking a stand and making a step towards a vision we may not see yet.

God is constantly trying to breathe a breath of inspiration into us with His questions. His promptings are designed to lead us in the direction of His promises. And yet instead of giving him an honest and bold answer, far too often, we claim it's complicated. We run and hide and go silent. Just like Allie, we make it complicated. I'm pretty sure Noah knew what Allie truly wanted. The Lord knows what we truly want. But without Allie using her voice and without us using our voice the vision we are designed to live cannot be activated.

What do you want? Stop making it complicated. Stop running and hiding. Stop silencing yourself. Burst the veil. Let your God-designed color splatter all over the canvas. Even if the splatter makes a mess. Because at least in the splatter, your color will begin to leave the right mark.

How did Achsah respond?

Achsah asks for two things: a blessing and for more than what she'd already received. Achsah's first ask is not a paternal declaration where Caleb lays hands on her and says: "You are blessed, my child." She's asking for an inheritance, a possession, a gift from her father. Something we've typically only seen happen between fathers and sons in this patriarchal society. She's asking for something tangible to be given. "Give me a blessing." Achsah doesn't stop there. (Caleb certainly activated her courageous conviction!) Notice what she says next: "Since you have given me the Negeb, give me also springs of water." Many commentators argue this ask comes from an ungrateful daughter. I don't hear Achsah that way. In fact, I hear the gratitude and acknowledgment that she knows her father, Caleb, gave her a great portion of land and that he has more to give. She courageously asks for more out of a deep sense of intimate knowing of what her father was able and wanted to give.

Isn't this what our Heavenly Father wants from us? For us to ask for blessings out of an intimate knowing that He has given to us, is able to give us, and wants to give us immeasurably more. When Caleb asks the question, "What do you want?" and activates Achsah's voice, her responses reveals her faith in her father. Her belief in the vision that the Lord had for Caleb and her awareness that what was given to him was only a partial fulfillment, but there was more. There was more for her to obtain and to add her voice to the indelible marks of Caleb's legacy.

When you answer the Lord's question, "What do you want?" how does your answer reveal your faith in His promises? How does your answer connect to the vision that He has for your life - that you may not see, but is who you were always meant to be? How does your answer reveal an activation of your God-designed color?

There's something else about Achsah's asks worth noting. She doesn't just ask generally for more. She asks with specificity. She asks specifically for springs of water. Achsah's knew the land of the Negeb was extremely dry land. If the vision of possessing the Promised Land was going to be sustained, they needed a water source. To this dry canvas of land, Achsah was adding bold blue waters to the masterpiece. This specific ask would sustain this family's possession of the Promised Land. Achsah's specificity reveals a strategy for staying tenacious in the tension between God's promises and their fulfillment. Know the nature of promise and ask for what you need to sustain the promise. Achsah knew the quality of the blessing she had received. She knew what her family needed in order to sustain the blessing - springs of water.

This is a reflection for us about what it means to collaborate with God in the tension and stewarding the vision He's given us to leave the right marks. Because Achsah activated her voice and asked specifically for springs of water, she added her color to the promise that her family would possess the Promised Land. Without her bold blue voice, those bold blue waters, may not have been part of the legacy. With her voice, she added the right mark - the right color - to God's canvas and it was a game changer. The Lord creates you with your God-designed color, but you activate your God-designed color. He gives you the freedom and opportunity to add your color to the canvas or not. He invites you to use that voice in a way that is specific and unique to you. In that specificity, you add the right marks to the canvas that will sustain you in the tension. Without your voice, the blessings the Lord has given you are in danger of drying out. They're in danger of losing the life and vitality through which they were given. When we respond to the Lord's question, "What do you want?" with specificity we are honoring His inspiration, by activating what's inside of us. We are releasing the breath of God in us, so that our voices are not asphyxiated. We breathe our voice back to Him and we activate the legacy. We don't simply activate the legacy for the future; we activate our voice to begin living the legacy now.

What do you want?
How will you respond?
Breathe in His inspiration.
Breathe out your response.

First Words

In Spanish, we have a word for Achsah's ask: atrevida. The closest English translation of this word is daring, but I always think of atrevida as something more. It's daring boldness. I want to be atrevida, like Achsah, in my asks of God. If I believe that he is able to do abundantly more than all I can ask or think according to His power at work in me[69], then I want to ask and think to the fullness of my capacity. I want to activate my voice to the fullness of its power - His power made perfect in me. I want to ask for more, like Achsah, knowing that God is able to give me more than what I ask for.

Achsah's ask incarnates the spiritual truth that God is able to give more. The story continues with Caleb not just giving his daughter springs of water, but giving her the upper springs AND the lower springs.[70] He gave abundantly more than asked. He gave her double the springs. I wonder if Caleb knew that for her to continue to possess the land, she was going to need more than she realized. She needs the springs of water in the north and the south. I wonder if this was Caleb's way of continuing the Lord's promise. The blessing of these springs of water - in the north and the south, in the high parts of the mountain range and the low parts of the mountain range - was an act of abundant provision. These springs would sustain Achsah's and her family in the tension between God's promises and their fulfillment. This special blessing was a continuation of the legacy.

This conversation between Caleb and Achsah is the last time we hear from Caleb. These words are the final right marks of Caleb's color on the canvas of God's masterpiece. These words are the first right marks of Achsah's on the canvas. In a brief, yet powerful, conversation, the legacy the Lord carried on through Caleb would now be carried on through Achsah. Just like Caleb and Achsah, we are carriers of a movement that God began in the beginning. It's bigger than us and yet God chooses us to be vessels of the legacy. In our voice - our God-designed color - the legacy moves from generation to generation. And each generation will leave a mark that is unique to the carrier. Achsah learned a lot from her father about finding her voice, but she carries the legacy with her God-designed color that was different from Caleb's. The way we carry the legacy in our voices is unique to us. The important thing to know is that we carry it and we steward what we carry by using our voice to inspire others, to activate others, and to continue the movement through others.

David puts it this way in one of his worship songs:

"One generation shall commend your works to another,
and shall declare your mighty acts.
On the glorious splendor of your majesty,
and on your wondrous works,
I will meditate.

They shall speak of the might of your awesome deeds,
and I will declare your greatness." [Psalm 145:4-6]

This is how we carry the legacy in our voices. This is how we spark
the potential in others to carry the legacy. This is how we inspire,
activate, and continue the legacy. We add an indelible mark to the
canvas, by using our voices to declare the greatness of God.

Endings Beginnings

In 2008, when I first started serving in youth ministry at the
church I was attending at the time, we were nomads. For the years
that would follow, we moved from place to place - basements and
classrooms. I even led bible studies in hallways and elevators. I
always joked that just like Mary and Joseph, there was no room
for us at the inn. In those days, we got creative and I learned a lot
about thinking outside the box for church.

The church was out-growing the original sanctuary and broke
ground on building a new sanctuary building. During the four
years of building the new sanctuary, the Lord put in my heart
to start a worship experience on Sundays as a training ground
to teach our young people how to both be in a service and lead a
service. This worship experience was aimed towards young people
and coordinated by young people. But with limited space, we had
to get creative with how to make this vision come to life.

The English Ministry, which had outgrown its space, began using
the basement of the original sanctuary during the 9AM Spanish-
speaking service. We had outgrown our spaces, so we followed
their lead and had our worship experience during the 12PM
Spanish-speaking service. This set up came with its challenges
and a lot of sweat equity to make a full worship experience come

to life, but with all hands on-deck we transformed the basement space to make it work.

I will never despise the days of small beginnings. Some of my best ministry memories are sitting on the floor in a circle with middle schoolers singing songs off of printed copies of lyrics. The set up and break down of this arrangement was challenging and exhausting, but we made the best of it.

It was Christmas of 2013 and I left to go home to Florida for the holidays. With no indication, when I returned for the New Year's Eve service, the service was being held in the new sanctuary. This was a big move for the whole congregation. The implications of this felt even bigger for the English ministry and the youth ministry, because it meant that we would now be able to use the original sanctuary.

In January 2014, we held our first worship experience in the original sanctuary. I was convinced I was dreaming. For the six years, I had been serving in youth ministry with this community, this was a blessing beyond what I ever imagined. As I preached for the first time in the original sanctuary, I had an out of body experience watching myself. I remembered a prayer from ten years earlier before going to college when my plans for my life looked very different. I was standing in the church where I grew up during an altar call. One of the pastor's sons prayed for me. He held up my hands and told me that I would stand in front of young people on altar in a church preaching. At the time, in my head I thought this guy is talking to the wrong person. This prayer is for someone to my right or to my left, but it's definitely not for me. In retrospect, I feel a little bit like the Biblical Sarah when she laughed about having Isaac at such an old age, because it was so impossible and not part of her and Abraham's plans. I had a plan. A law school plan. Not a preach to young people plan.

That prophetic prayer was impossible. Fast forward to our first worship experience in the original sanctuary. I stood in front of young people on an altar in my church preaching about God.

I continued preaching and having my out of body experience watching myself, when another memory flashed through my mind. A couple years earlier, just below where I now stood, the pastors and a few other key people in my ministry journey gathered around me, held up my hands (again, clearly a theme for me), and anointed me for ministry. They prayed that this moment would be my ordination moment into ministry. During that prayer, I never conceived that I would be the pastor overseeing the ministering in this space - at this altar. When I started going to that church in August 2008, I sat in that sanctuary listening to the senior pastor and other pastors preach from that altar. Back then, I would have told you this was an impossibility.

I preached every Sunday from the altar in the original sanctuary for four years. The Lord gave me an incredible gift of continuing the legacy of ministry that came from that altar for nearly twenty years. The gospel that has been shared from that altar by countless pastors and brothers and sisters from the church was a legacy I had the opportunity to continue. Even though, I stood in front of people teaching the Bible for several years at that point, that first worship experience was the day I started to find my preaching voice. It was the day that I started to add my unique color to this part of the legacy that I carried inside of me. I didn't preach like others who preached from that altar. I brought my God-designed color to preaching. Sometimes my color was a yellow splattered all over the canvas and sometimes it was a well-defined yellow. But it was my voice, stewarding the opportunity to carry the legacy of God in the original sanctuary. It was an honor. The church made an intentional decision to not call it the "old sanctuary" and I'm thankful for that, because for me, it became my original starting place - the place where my preaching voice originated.

There's one more special reality of the original sanctuary that I learned only a few month before our first worship experience. During the initial renovations to the original sanctuary, twenty years earlier, they discovered the sanctuary was built on water. Many of the old buildings in Boston are built on water and have to be fortified in special ways, so that they don't sink. I think God planted that fun fact in my consciousness a few months before our first worship experience for a purpose. When God's timing came for me to share His word with our young people in this building built on water, I would feel empowered knowing this place was fortified not to sink. I would feel empowered knowing the Lord who is living water would sustain His vision for me in this place. This place of special blessing, much like what Achsah received, was a place where I was able to inspire, to activate, and to continue the movement.

Indelible Marks

Achsah continues the legacy of her father, Caleb. Even though her voice doesn't enter the biblical story again, the life of her husband, Caleb's nephew - Othniel, does enter the story. The legacy continues in the book of Judges when the Israelites became disobedient to the Lord and served other gods. Their disobedience led the Lord to allow them to be sold into slavery to serve another king. This was a wakeup call for the Israelites! They cried out to the Lord to deliver them from the oppression of this king.

> "...the Lord raised up a deliverer for the people of Israel, who saved them, Othniel the son of Kenaz, Caleb's younger brother. The Spirit of the Lord

was upon him, and he judged Israel. He went out to war, and the Lord gave Cushan-rishathaim king of Mesopotamia into his hand. And his hand prevailed over Cushan-rishathaim. So the land had rest forty years." [Judges 3:9b-11]

After Joshua passed away and the Israelites had turned away from the Lord, Othniel was the first judge in Israel. Much like his Uncle Caleb, when everyone else was led by fear over faith, he remained faithful. Othniel's faith led him to become the leader the people of Israel needed in a time of deep distress. I wonder if Othniel heard his Uncle Caleb tell stories of God's faithfulness to bring him and Joshua from wandering in the wilderness to possessing the Promised Land. I wonder if his wife Achsah and Othniel recounted those stories to their children about the faithfulness of God and their Grandpa Caleb. We can only speculate, but I imagine the legacy carried in the voice of Caleb and in the voice of Achsah inspired, activated, and continued the movement the Lord gave through this family tree. One generation commending the works of God to the next generation. The legacy of faithfulness leaving an indelible mark on the canvas of Israel's history.

Who knows whether Caleb was thinking about how his God-designed color would leave an indelible mark of inspiration that would activate other colors and continue God's masterpiece. Who knows if he knew that his voice carried a legacy that would be catalytic for the voices in others? We don't know. What we do know is that we've gone on a journey with Caleb through this book and his voice is still leaving the right marks, because it's left a mark on all of us. God wanted to uncover something in Caleb, so that He could work through Caleb to reach you - to inspire you to activate your voice and continue the masterpiece. Let Caleb's last words: "What do you want?" spark something powerful in you. Choose to respond with courageous conviction to the vision

God has given you. Let your voice - even if it splatters all over the canvas - leave an indelible mark that both carries the legacy and carries on in the tension between God's promises and their fulfillment.

Color You _____ Moment

Questions to Ponder:
- If you sat down for coffee or tea or ice cream (or whatever you enjoy consuming!) and God asked you, "what do you want", how would you respond?
- Knowing that God is able to do immeasurably more than we could ever ask, how can you use your voice to speak into existence the legacy that God is moving through you?
- Looking back over the past few weeks or months, how would you describe the mark your voice is leaving on those around you?

Coloring Exercise: What Are Your Indelible Marks?
An indelible mark is an imprint that is enduring and cannot be forgotten. Caleb's indelible mark impacted his daughter in a way that influenced her voice and future. Our voices have the power to leave this kind of impact and create this kind of influence.

- Write a poem, compose a song, draw a picture, write a journal entry, create a mashup of these different mediums, or create something different to express your indelible mark.
  - What's your big ask of God?
  - What and/or who will you impact?
  - What will you impact them to do or be?

FINDING YOUR VOICE

"De qué me sirve la vida
Si no la vivo contigo
De que me valen mis pasos
Si no caminas conmigo
Quiero quedarme a tu lado
Tu amor es lo que te pido
De qué me sirve la vida
Si no la vivo contigo" // Musiko, Anexo

"Of what value is my life
if I don't live it with you
Of what value are my steps
If I you don't walk with me
I want to stay by your side
Your love is all I ask
Of what value is my life
If I don't live it with you" // Musiko, Anexo

What if I told you that the "your" in "finding your voice in the tension between God's promises and their fulfillment" is actually God? We cannot find our voice, if we have not first found God's voice. He is the primary "your" and we reflect what we've found in Him.

> "For I have not spoken on my own authority, but the Father who sent me has himself given me a commandment - what to say and what to speak. And I know that his commandment is eternal life. What I say, therefore, I say as the Father has told me." [John 12:49-50]

Even Jesus understood that the words He was speaking did not come from him, but they came from His Father. Jesus - the Messiah, the one who was God with skin on - spoke with a voice that was not His own. He understood that the authority in his voice came from God's voice. And more than that, He understood that his voice - His God-designed color - was commissioned by God for an eternal purpose.

You may be thinking, well I'm not Jesus. And yet, you are called to be transformed into his image and likeness for the sake of God's glory.[71] You may be thinking, I'm not commissioned by God for eternal purposes. And yet, you are given the instructions to go and make disciples.[72] What makes this instruction the "Great Commission" is because of its eternal implications. So, if Jesus found God's voice and spoke according to God's words, how much more do we need to find God's voice to speak according to His words. God gave us access to his voice in many ways and most explicitly through the Word.

I come from a family of Bible teachers. My father taught theology. My mother started teaching Sunday School as a teenager and continues to teach people how to practically connect with scripture. My Abuela - frail as she was in her last days with eyes that could barely read the Bible anymore - taught Sunday School at her small mountainside church in Puerto Rico. My grandfather gathered his children together to study the Bible. I could go on and on and tell you of others in my family who led and lead others to hear God's voice by teaching the Word.

Late one night in the hospital, during one of the last conversations with my papa, we talked about how to communicate the Word of God to a generation who doesn't like to read. How can we inspire people to read the Word of God and hear the voice of God in His words?

Don't get excited! We didn't come to any conclusions in our conversation. But our conversation led me to a commitment: to teach people why the Bible is essential to finding their voice and to guide others in learning to read and understand the Bible to find the voice of God and find their voice in Him. This commitment is in many ways a footnote to a line in my personal vision statement: build people up to become the God-designed version of themselves and to fulfill their specific calling. It's a footnote that I mention, because of the incredible relevance to our journey together in finding our voices. I pray that as I've modeled the ways I dig into God's word to draw out His voice, you've seen how the Bible can come alive when you dig. I want to seize the opportunity in this last chapter of our journey together to use my yellow voice to shine a light on why finding the voice of God in His Word is essential to finding your voice and learning to read and understand the voice of God in the Word of God.

God's Truths > Your Feelings

We live in a culture that celebrates "doing what feels good to you" and "you do you." These mantras are not inherently bad. The challenge with celebrating these mantras comes when what feels good to you on the surface is harmful to your soul. It comes when "you doing you" results in you doing something offensive to someone else, because they don't look like you, talk like you, or think like you. These mantras, while seeming to come from a sincere place of celebrating our unique individuality and voices, can cause us to become disintegrated with ourselves and with each other. They can cause us to distort truth, because we're gratifying what's temporary and not what's eternal. In an attempt to honor uniqueness, feelings supersede truth and truth becomes an illusion grounded in the feelings of today that are gone tomorrow.

As humans, we've been doing this since the beginning of existence. God gives us a clear word and we twist it to gratify our temporary feelings. God told Adam and Eve that they could not eat from the tree of the knowledge of good and evil. Then, the snake corners Eve to ask: "Did God actually say you couldn't eat from any tree in the garden?"[73] This is clearly not what the Lord told her, but the snake's subtle deception starts to get Eve all twisted and she "does her" by eating from the tree to satisfy what's temporary. Before we get judge-y and blame Eve for the fall of humankind, we can all fall into this subtle trap as we're "doing what feels good" to us in the moment.

I struggle with allowing truth to be louder than my feelings. I never realized how much I struggle with this until a friend said to me: "When did your feelings about what you think I think, become louder than my truths about what I know I think." That was one of the hardest things anyone has ever said to me. But true friends call you out, so you don't get the truth twisted. And when she said that to me, I realized that I was being led by my feelings and letting my feelings twist the truth.

We do this in our interactions with people and in our interactions with God. We can allow our immediate feelings to be louder than God's timeless truths. When we're in the midst of our lives our feelings are immediate and we want to satisfy what's most immediate. But feelings are temporary. Our journey together has taught us that finding our voice is not about satisfying what's temporary. We've learned that finding our voice is about being tenacious for the long-term.

Jesus illustrates being tenacious for the truth when He's confronted in the wilderness after fasting for 40 days. He could have allowed His immediate feelings to be louder than God's timeless truths, but He doesn't. This scene in Matthew 4 comes on the heels of a glorious moment after John the Baptist baptizes Jesus and the Spirit of God descends on Him like a dove with a voice from heaven crying out: "This is my beloved Son, with whom I am well pleased."[74] This is a clear affirmation of the truth of God being declared over Jesus. That scene ends and the narrative picks up again with the Spirit leading Jesus into the wilderness to be tempted by the devil. Not unlike Eve's encounter with the snake, Satan attempts to deceive Jesus and exploit His immediate feelings by telling him to turn stones to bread. Jesus responds:

> "It is written, 'Man shall not live by bread alone,
> but by every word that comes from the mouth of
> God.'" [Matthew 4:4]

Take that Satan! Take that immediate feelings of hunger! In my own journey, these words from Jesus have given me clarity about why the Word of God is essential to finding my voice for three reasons:

1. God's Word is a Timeless Truth: Jesus, after being in the wilderness fasting for 40 days and 40 nights, was probably hungry. Jesus had the power to turn the stones into bread. But he doesn't act on the commands of Satan to satisfy

a temporary feeling. Jesus acts on the timeless truths of every word that comes from the mouth of God.

2. God's Word is the Life-Source: Jesus isn't interested in mere survival; He's interested in living fully alive. When He says: "man shall not live" this "living" means the fullness of life, the possessing of life, the aliveness that comes from connection to the true life-source. A life-source that cannot be found in temporary feelings.

3. God's Word is Eternal: Jesus quotes these words from the Old Testament. Jesus understands that everything fades away, but the power and truth of the word of God lasts forever.[75] So, He doesn't have to quote himself, He can quote what's eternal to overcome what's temporary.

And here's a bonus! When we dig into where Jesus quotes from in the Old Testament, we come back to Deuteronomy. If you remember back to the "Color You _____" Chapter, you'll remember that we discovered that Deuteronomy is a book about remembrance. Moses writes to a community embarking on a journey into the Promised Land and he wants them to remember certain timeless truths. We learned that the word "remember" in Hebrew is zakar meaning to bring past events to mind in a way that causes them to impact present feelings, thoughts, and actions. I wonder if Jesus - the Word made flesh - quotes from Deuteronomy, because in his wilderness moment where His feelings could have gotten the best of Him, he needed to remember. He needed to remember how the Lord brought the Israelites into the promise and the Lord would bring Him into the promise. I wonder if despite the circumstances and how hungry he must have been, speaking these words of God empowered Him to silence His immediate feelings and trust God's timeless truths.

We will end up in the wilderness. That may not sound super encouraging, but it's the truth. Some days I wake up, I've prayed in the shower, I've worshipped while making my coffee, I've set my intentions for a great day, and then 11:30AM happens. Something happens to make feel frustrated, annoyed, and dried out not knowing what to do. Hello again, wilderness! My feelings feel loud. I'm tempted to lead with my feelings, but then I remind myself to remember the timeless truths of God. I remember that God gave me His Word filled with timeless truths. I remember that God's desire for me is to live fully alive. I remember that my voice on its own is insensitive, obnoxious, and critical.

All these reminders of God's timeless truths lead me to recognizing the only way that I make it to the promise - to the good land that God is still bringing me into - is to live by God's words and speak by God's words.

God is still bringing you into the Promised Land. Our Color Me journey has taught us that on this side of eternity we will see the fulfillment of the promises of God, but it's a partial fulfillment. Because God is still bringing us into the fullness of His promise, we urgently need His word to ground us. When we allow the Word of God to ground us, we have eternal truth to guide us. If God's Word was a faithful guide to the Israelites and to Jesus, then why wouldn't His Word be a faithful guide to us as we find and speak our voices in the tension between God's promises and their fulfillment?

Living the Greatest Love Story

I watched a young person solve a rubix cube like he was the superhero, the Flash. I asked him, where did you learn to solve a rubix cube so fast? His response: YouTube. The tone in his voice suggested this was clearly an obvious answer! I may be dating myself a bit, but I grew up thinking YouTube was reserved for music videos. And hadn't really used it for much else. However, I'm quickly learning that you can learn how to do anything on YouTube. I just typed in "how to" in the search bar on YouTube and here's a list of the first things that popped up:

How to make slime
How to make slime without glue
How to tie a tie
How to basic
How to draw
How to make fluffy slime
How to make slime without borax
How to kiss

Apparently a lot of people want to learn how to make slime! Our society has the greatest access to "how to" do just about anything through YouTube. We have quick and easy step-by-step videos to learn how to do just about anything, which is both beautiful and complicated. Beautiful, because we can learn so many new things all the time. I learned how to skateboard watching YouTube videos. Complicated, because it can create a mindset that everything can be learned and understood in a 3-minute step-by-step video. And while you may be excited to read this section on learning to read and understand the Bible to find the voice of God and your voice, I need to let you in on a disclaimer. Learning to read and understand the Word is less about "how to" and more about "how do."

How do you perceive the Word of God?
How do you see God in His words?
How do you see yourself through His words?

Learning to read and understand the Bible is ultimately a reflection of how you perceive the Bible. The Word of God is a gift meant to be received by us. It's alive, so that we can come to life. How you perceive the Word of God impacts whether you can fully receive the word of God. Whether or not you can receive His voice speaking to you impacts whether you can receive and speak your voice.

Let me wear my lawyer hat for a moment to shed some light on how we can learn to read and understand the Word of God. The Bible is divided into two parts: the Old Testament and the New Testament. These two parts are better translated as the Old Covenant and the New Covenant. Understanding the legal and biblical concepts of covenants shifts how we perceive the Word of God.

A covenant is a type of contract. It forms a relationship between two parties: a covenanter and a covenantee. In the relationship, the covenanter makes a promise and the convenantee is the person who benefits from the promise. Covenants are used in property law as conditions attached to property rights.

The Lord uses the concept of a covenant to establish a relationship between Himself and Abram. In Genesis, the Lord tells Abram:

> "Go from your country and your kindred and your father's house to the land that I will show you. And I will make you a great nation, and I will bless you and make your name great, so that you will be a blessing. I will bless those who bless you, and him who dishonors you I will curse and in you all the families of the earth shall be blessed… Look to the heaven, and number the stars, if you are able to number them…So shall your offspring be…I am the Lord who brought you out from Ur

of the Chaldeans to give you this land to possess."
[Genesis 12:1-3, 15:5, 7]

The Lord enters into this covenant relationship with Abram.
God tells Abram that He's going to give him land, to make him
a great nation, to bless him and his name to be a blessing, to give
him innumerable offspring, and to allow him to possess the land
he's given him.

In addition to the promise of the covenanter to the covenantee,
there is something given in exchange from the covenantee. In
the ancient world in order to seal covenants, they cut animals
in half to set up a pathway that the covenantee walked through.
This represented the covenantee's commitment not to break the
covenant relationship and the promise that was made. If the
conventee's commitment was broken, they would be cut in half
just like the animals.

We see this ancient covenantal tradition between God and Abram:

> "But he [Abram] said, "O Lord God, how am I
> to know that I shall possess it?" He said to him,
> "Bring me a heifer three years old, a female goat
> three year old, a ram three year old, a turtledove,
> and a young pigeon." And he brought him all
> these, cut them in half and laid each half over
> against the other...
>
> As the sun was going down, a deep sleep fell on
> Abram. And behold a dreadful and great darkness
> fell upon him. Then the Lord said to Abram,
> "Know for certain that your offspring will be
> sojourners in a land that is not theirs and will be
> servants there, and they will be afflicted for four

hundred years. But I will bring judgment on the nation that they serve, and afterward they shall come out with great possessions. As for you, you shall go to your fathers in peace, you shall be buried in a good old age. And they shall come back here in the fourth generation, for the iniquity of the Amorites is not yet complete."

When the sun had gone down and it was dark, behold, a smoking fire pot and a flaming torch passed between the pieces. On that day the Lord made a covenant with Abram, saying, To your offspring I give this land from the river of Egypt to the great river, the river Euphrates, the land of the Kenites, the Kenizzites, the Kadmonites, the Hittites, the Perizzites, the Rephaim, the Amorites, the Canaanites, the Girgashites and the Jebusites." [Genesis 15:8-10, 12-21]

What is distinct from customary covenant traditions is the way the covenant relationship between the Lord and Abram is sealed. Instead of Abram (as the covenantee) walking through the pathway of the cut up animals, the smoking fire pot and flaming torch pass through the pathway. These miraculous wonders are representations of the Lord. The Lord takes on the burden of the commitment, if the covenant is broken. Essentially, God will take on the punishment - being cut in half.

This Bible that God has given us is a covenant. It is the story of the relationship that the eternal God wants to enter into with you. A relationship where He promises that you will possess the Promised Land. Unlike the typical requirements of covenants, God carries the commitment to bring the promise into fulfillment on Himself. When your sins break the covenant, He bears the punishment. The incarnation of God, Jesus - the word made flesh, bore our punishment when He went to the cross. When Jesus took the punishment on, he became "the mediator of a new covenant, so that those who are called may receive the promised eternal inheritance, since a death has occurred that redeems them from the transgression committed under the first covenant."[76]

The Word of God is the story of our covenantal relationship with God. The Word of God invites us to connect with God. This connection is not about learning helpful "how to" information; the connection is about receiving the gift of revelation. The gift of revelation is of who He truly is and who we truly are in Him. When you perceive the words of God this way, you begin to see the adventure of this love story on every page. You begin living the adventure of every spoken word.

I have a friend who once said, "I'm thankful that I don't have to want to have a love story, because I'm already living the greatest love story." When you perceive the Word of God as words from God who relentlessly pursues you with His eternal love, the more you see yourself as fully loved. We go searching for love in so many places and people. But in the Word of God we're given permission to stop searching and to be found by the Eternal Lover.

The Eternal Lover finds us and His words never return empty, because he never breaks His pinky promises to us.[77]

The Eternal Lover finds us and His words reads us, refines us, and redefines us.[78]

The Eternal Lover finds us and His words become a map that lead us to prosperity.[79]

The Eternal Lover finds us and His words show us how we find our true God-design and proclaim our God-designed voice.[80]

Be found in Him.
Be found in His words.
Be found in His voice.

In His voice, you find your voice in the tension between God's promises and their fulfillment.

Color You _____ Moment

Coloring Exercise: Drawing Our Love Story
- Draw a picture of how you see God in light of this chapter
- Draw yourself into that picture
- Reflect on...
  - What colors did I use?
  - What images did I use?
  - How am I a reflection of how I see God?
  - How do I want to be a reflection of how I see God?
- Share your picture and the answers to these questions with someone

EPILOGUE: THE MUSIC CONTINUES...

This book isn't for you.

I started writing this book as a personal exercise. Yes, I'm deeply devoted to supporting others on the journey of finding their voices. Many of the foundational themes came from a series I originally did with the young people I was pastoring. But this book wasn't about supporting others as much as it was about reflecting and healing that I needed. A creative process of uncovering, refining, and strengthening my voice that I needed to engage in before stepping in to the next season of my story.

This creative process took three years. These years have probably been the three most painful years of my life so far. And yet, through the pain, I painted on the empty canvas of Pages on my laptop. In this creative process, the music that I thought stopped, started to play again. It started to play again, because I learned that my gray needs my yellow and my yellow needs my gray.

The editing process alone took me about a year. I experienced more transitions in my life during the year of editing than I could have ever predicted. There were days you could only color me gray. Other days, the gray and yellow were complimentary colors. Through the editing process, I felt as though I was editing my own colors. People asked me: "How's the editing going?" My response was the same every time: "If I wrote this book only to support me, it's doing its work."

When I needed it the most, the words that we've just finished reading together comforted me and confronted me. When I felt like the future was bright, these words strengthened me. When I I felt lost, these words corrected me.

You hold in your hands the color I'm only beginning to add to the canvas of God's masterpiece. The color that, as you've probably discovered, has many different shades. Sometimes you've heard my pastoral voice. Sometimes you've heard my friend voice. Sometimes you've heard my coaching voice. You too have many different, and beautiful, shades of your color. I need the color you bring to the canvas, because together our colors are creating something beautiful.

Finding our voices is a deeply personal journey. We uncover, refine, and strengthen. But that process comes through excavation, through fire, and through discipline. And then, there's the choice we make to express our voices, which comes at the cost of critique and criticism. This is a deeply personal journey.

This book isn't for you, because sharing the voice you've found empowers others to speak. This book isn't for you to keep your voice to yourself. This book is for you to share your voice with others. To paint on the canvas. To invite others to paint with you. To make room for their colors, so that together we add our colors to God's masterpiece on earth.

My prayer is that my last words, will be your first words. My last splashes of yellow, will be your first colors on the canvas of God's masterpiece.

Let's start coloring together!

Rebeca Villatoro, one of the young people who inspired the original Color Me Journey and who I am honored to color alongside, in her own words:

"Color me green.
Green, the way this color mixes with other colors to illuminate the shade, tones, and hues of God's creation.
Green, the way a thorn embraces and protects a white roses' purity.
Green, the way resilient trees die to themselves during the winter to blossom in the spring.
Green, the way a cloud's cry gives vibrancy to dry grass.
Green, the way tenacious roots tether one's identity to fortify authenticity.
Green, the way a planter sows seeds of love, influence, and vision in those they serve.
Color me a shade that grows branches to create a home for the tired and weary to rest.
Color me green." // Rebeca Villatoro

ENDNOTES

1   Ephesians 2:6
2   Romans 12:2
3   Ephesians 2:10
4   Numbers 14:33
5   Matthew 24:35
6   STRONGS NT 3056
7   John 6:35
8   John 4:14
9   Hebrews 4:12
10   Psalm 119:105
11   Being asked by the Pharisees when the kingdom of God would come, he answered them, "The kingdom of God is not coming in ways that can be observed, nor will they say, 'Look, here it is!' or 'There!' for behold, the kingdom of God is in the midst of you." Luke 17:20-21
12   Just like the fearful Israelites in Numbers 14:33
13   Luke 1:37
14   Hebrews 11:1
15   Numbers 13:30
16   Numbers 13:30
17   Numbers 13:33
18   Exodus 33:18-23
19   He linked the story of Moses with a woman who dealt with chronic menstrual bleeding for twelve years. She sees Jesus walking through a crowd of folks and because she heard of the stories about how Jesus healed people, she thought to herself: "If I could just touch his clothes, I'd be healed. So, she reaches out to touch Jesus's clothes and in the crowd of people, Jesus realized someone touched Him and healing power went out of him. Jesus turns around in the crowd asking: "Who

237

touched me?" At this turning around, this woman saw the glory of God in the face of Jesus. She experienced a greater glory than Moses and so do we. Mark 5:25-34

20 2 Corinthians 12:9

21 Exodus 3:8

22 Job 1-2

23 Job 19:25

24 "But my servant Caleb, because he has a different spirit and has followed me fully, I will bring into the land into which he went, and his descendants shall possess it." [Numbers 14:24]

25 Proverbs 29:18

26 "I am the Lord your God, who brought you out of the land of Egypt to be your God: I am the Lord your God." [Numbers 15:41]

27 "And the Lord said to Moses, 'Put back the staff of Aaron before the testimony to be kept as a sign for the rebels, that you may make an end of their grumblings against me, lest they die.'" [Numbers 17:10]

28 Numbers 16:3

29 Exodus 30:34-38

30 "And the incense that you shall make according to its composition, you shall not make for yourselves. It shall be for you holy to the Lord." Exodus 30:37

31 Numbers 16:38

32 Numbers 3:27

33 Numbers 3:28-31

34 If we look at the Reubenites family tree, we see that Reuben was the firstborn son of Jacob/Israel. The rights of the father always belonged to the firstborn in this culture. In addition, the priestly role in the family belonged to the firstborn. But even though Reuben was the firstborn, because he was "unstable as water" he would have no leadership among the family. Reuben was passed over for the priestly role in favor of the fourth son, Levi. Dathan, Abiram, and On were overlooked and unseen just like Korah. Although it was in a different way, they shared the common thread - and arguably a common wound - of a family whose expectations were unmet and who may have felt unseen by God.

35 Numbers 16:11

36 Numbers 16:15

37 Numbers 16:3

38 Numbers 16:28

39 Exodus 30:26-29

40 Exodus 30:34-38
41 Leviticus 11:44; 1 Peter 1:16
42 Matthew 11:30
43 Numbers 25:1
44 Numbers 25:4
45 Numbers 25:3
46 Numbers 25:11
47 Numbers 25:14
48 Numbers 25:11
49 1 Peter 2:5, 9
50 Joshua 13:1
51 Ephesians 6:10-20
52 I can't take credit for the descriptions for each day. They are the powerful voice of my friend, Paula. I pray you all have friends that will stand alongside you in the tension as you find your voice. I pray that you will have priestly trailblazers in your life whose color enhances your color. She took my all-over-the-place voice and helped refine them into concrete ideas that we could pray and fast over in the days leading up to my resignation.
53 https://www.studylight.org/commentaries/rbc/joshua-14.html?print=yes
54 Numbers 34:19
55 Joshua 14:11
56 http://www.bible-archaeology.info/bible_city_hebron.htm
57 Joshua 14:14
58 Numbers 13:22
59 Numbers 26:11
60 1 Chronicles 6:33
61 1 Chronicles 6:33, 1 Chronicles 25:5
62 Romans 4:17b
63 1 Peter 1:3b
64 Romans 4:18
65 Exodus 33:18
66 Proverbs 18:21a
67 Joshua 15:17
68 1 Chronicles 4:15
69 Ephesians 3:20
70 Joshua 15:19b
71 2 Corinthians 3:18

72   Matthew 28:10

73   Genesis 3:1

74   Matthew 3:16-17

75   Matthew 24:35

76   Hebrews 9:15

77   Isaiah 55:10-11

78   2 Timothy 3:16-17

79   Joshua 1:8

80   1 Peter 2:9-10